TRACING YOUR NAVAL ANCESTORS

FAMILY HISTORY FROM PEN & SWORD BOOKS

Tracing Your Channel Islands Ancestors
Marie-Louise Backhurst

Tracing Your Yorkshire Ancestors
Rachel Bellerby

Tracing Your Royal Marine Ancestors
Richard Brooks and Matthew Little

Tracing Your Pauper Ancestors
Robert Burlison

Tracing Your Labour Movement Ancestors
Mark Crail

Tracing Your Army Ancestors
Simon Fowler

A Guide to Military History on the Internet
Simon Fowler

Tracing Your Northern Ancestors
Keith Gregson

Your Irish Ancestors
Ian Maxwell

Tracing Your Scottish Ancestors
Ian Maxwell

Tracing Your London Ancestors
Jonathan Oates

Tracing Your Air Force Ancestors
Phil Tomaselli

Tracing Your Secret Service Ancestors
Phil Tomaselli

Tracing Your Criminal Ancestors
Stephen Wade

Tracing Your Police Ancestors
Stephen Wade

Tracing Your Jewish Ancestors
Rosemary Wenzerul

Fishing and Fishermen
Martin Wilcox

TRACING YOUR NAVAL ANCESTORS

A Guide for Family Historians

SIMON FOWLER

Pen & Sword
FAMILY HISTORY

First published in Great Britain in 2011 by
PEN AND SWORD FAMILY HISTORY
an imprint of
Pen & Sword Books Ltd
47 Church Street
Barnsley
South Yorkshire
S70 2AS

Copyright © Simon Fowler 2011

ISBN 978 1 84884 625 8

A CIP catalogue record for this book is
available from the British Library

Typeset in 10pt Palatino by Mac Style, Beverley, East Yorkshire
Printed and bound in the UK by CPI

Pen & Sword Books Ltd incorporates the Imprints of Pen & Sword
Aviation, Pen & Sword Family History, Pen & Sword Maritime, Pen
& Sword Military, Pen & Sword Discovery, Wharncliffe Local History,
Wharncliffe True Crime, Wharncliffe Transport, Pen & Sword Select,
Pen & Sword Military Classics, Leo Cooper, The Praetorian Press,
Remember When, Seaforth Publishing and Frontline Publishing.

For a complete list of Pen & Sword titles please contact
PEN & SWORD BOOKS LIMITED
47 Church Street, Barnsley, South Yorkshire, S70 2AS, England
E-mail: enquiries@pen-and-sword.co.uk
Website: www.pen-and-sword.co.uk

CONTENTS

PREFACE

Before I began writing this book I have to say that I didn't know very much about records of the Royal Navy. Indeed they rather scared me because they were so different to the records of the Army and Royal Air Force, with which I was fairly familiar. But in fact my explorations have been fascinating. This book is an attempt to share my findings with you.

I hope you will find the voyage as enlightening. True, in general naval personnel and operational records are less informative than their Army equivalent. And record keeping, and the way that the records are arranged, can be confusing. But, in compensation, the records go back further than for the Army. Realistically, it is possible to find information about ancestors who served in the Navy of the 1670s and 1680s, which would be impossible for soldiers in the Army for the same period. And there are some superb online resources, particularly for the twentieth century.

Fortunately, like the War Office, the Admiralty (and its parts the Navy, Transport and Sick and Hurt boards) believed in bureaucracy. There are lots of very similar records, so if one set of documents is missing then there may well be a duplicate which will do almost as well. And almost everything was recorded in one way and another, so with a bit of delving and a slice of luck you might well be able to piece together a reasonably detailed picture of your ancestor's naval career. And this is becoming easier almost on a daily basis as new indexes are added to the online catalogue of The National Archives and the records themselves are being digitised and put online.

When I was a child I was told that I was descended from naval officers. Captain Osbertus Fowler was occasionally mentioned in hushed tones and his naval telescope was handed round at family gatherings. But he turns out to have been a merchant seaman, taking emigrants to Australia and his telescope was presented to him by grateful passengers after a particularly difficult voyage. On my grandmother's side there is a real-life naval captain, Henry Edward Crozier. His portrait in full dress uniform dominates my cousin's dining room. Again, family legend tied him to the ill-fated Franklin Expedition to the Arctic in the 1840s, but unfortunately this too is a myth. He seems to have ventured no further north than Orkney.

The Royal Navy has a fascinating history and fascinating records to explore and stories to follow up. And, of course, today's officers and rates continue to follow in the footsteps of the great seamen of the past, of whom your ancestors were almost certainly among their number.

Men gather around to listen to a yarn. (William Glasscock, *Naval Sketch Book* (1835))

ACKNOWLEDGEMENTS

I have received help from a number of sources. In particular Chris Donnithorne organised a visit to the Royal Naval Museum and Admiralty libraries and patiently answered a number of basic questions about naval historical research. And Melissa Gerbaldi, the press officer at Portsmouth Historic Dockyard, organised a press pass and provided some images for this book. Thanks also to Allison Wearley and her colleagues at the Royal Naval Museum Library and Jenny Wraight and Ian Mackenzie at the Naval Historical Branch and Admiralty Library, who showed me around and answered questions. More pictures and much advice came from Richard Taylor. Again, many thanks. Rupert Harding and his colleagues at Pen & Sword, who saw the book through the editorial process.

All errors and omissions of course are my own.

But no thanks to the person who stole my rucksack (with my notes) while I was on a research trip to Portsmouth. In the remote chance that he reads this, he should know that until the end of the eighteenth century the punishment for theft at sea was for the thief to 'run the gauntlet'. The offender first received a dozen lashes in the normal manner with a thieves' cat, with knots throughout the length of the cords, and while still stripped to the waist, passed through two lines of all the ship's company, to be flogged with short lengths of rope. Lest he move too fast to benefit fully from this ordeal, the master-at-arms marched backwards a pace ahead of him with the point of his cutlass against the thief's chest. And to prevent him stopping, a ship's corporal followed him in a similar manner. On completion of the course the thief was given a further dozen lashes. Seems about right to me!

GLOSSARY

It is inevitable that many terms and sources are repeated through the book without further explanation. To prevent unnecessary duplication and tedium among readers, here is a list:

ADM
Almost all the series of records relating to the Royal Navy and its personnel are to be found in this lettercode at The National Archives (ADM of course stands for Admiralty).

Ancestry
A commercial data provider at www.ancestry.co.uk.

Documents Online
The online records service provided by The National Archives at www.nationalarchives.gov.uk/documents online.

Findmypast
A commercial data provider at www.findmypast.co.uk.

Kew
The home of The National Archives.

Pappalardo
Bruno Pappalardo, *Tracing Your Naval Ancestors* (Public Record Office, 2002) – the most comprehensive guide to the records at Kew. If you are going to research your naval forebears in any detail you will need this book.

RN
Royal Navy.

ScotlandsPeople
A commercial data provider (Scottish records only) at www.scotlandspeople.gov.uk.

TNA
The National Archives.

In addition, you may occasionally come across a URL that looks something like http://tinyurl.com/2ej7p6e. It is a way of shortening very long Internet addresses – just type the phrase into your browser and it will take you to the webpage under discussion.

Chapter 1

GETTING STARTED

Where to Start

The best place to begin your research is to work out what you know already. Write down definite facts as well as anything about which you are not sure.

- The full name of the person you are researching, as well as any variants that you might be aware of. Your grandfather, known as Jack Tarre, might have enlisted as John Horatio Tarre or be in the records as J. H. Tarre or even have the name misspelled by the clerks as Jake Tar.
- Whether he was a commissioned officer, warrant officer or ordinary seaman or rating. This may be important as the records can be very different depending on a man's rank.
- The names of any ships he served on (there are likely to be several).
- When he enlisted (usually at about 18, but he may have been as young as 14) and when he was discharged.
- Date of death if killed in action or died of wounds.

Photographs of ancestors in naval uniform can often be very informative as the badges they are wearing can tell you a lot about their service. The sleeves of this seaman from the cruiser HMS Antrim are carefully arranged to display his badges. They show that he was a seaman gunner first class (Queen's crown above a gun). He was also a second class marksman, as indicated by the crossed rifles without the addition of a star. The medals are the Egypt Medal with clasp and the Khedive's Star, which invariably accompanied it. The medal was awarded to servicemen who took part in operations in Egypt and the Sudan between 1882 and 1889. The seaman also wears two good conduct badges on his left arm. The first was awarded for three years' very good conduct, the second for eight years. (Richard Taylor)

In an ideal world you would also know his:

- Service number.
- Rank (ordinary seaman, chief petty officer, lieutenant) and/or trade (wireless operator).
- Any medals he was awarded.

This book will help you follow up these leads and give you ideas about where else you might look for information. Once you start, you might be pleasantly surprised about what you can find out.

Background Research

It is a good idea to familiarise yourself with the period, and perhaps get a feel for the life experienced by your ancestor, by doing some background reading. There are a huge numbers of books on naval history, particularly for the two world wars, and I've included a selection at the end of this book.

You can find out what is currently in print by visiting the Amazon website (www.amazon.co.uk) and most bookshops can order any book currently in print for you – surprisingly, this is often cheaper and quicker than ordering via Amazon. For out of print books try Abebooks (www.abebooks.co.uk). There are also a number of booksellers who specialise in new or second-hand naval history. The Royal Naval Museum has posted a list of these at www.royalnavalmuseum.org/info_sheets_naval_booksellers.htm, although I suspect that it may be a little dated.

An increasing proportion of books have been digitised and are available online, including a surprising number of books about the Royal Navy and memoirs of old tars. For copyright reasons these are generally published before about 1930. The largest collections are at:

- http://books.google.co.uk – Google Books has scanned hundreds of thousands of books. Often an ordinary Google search will turn up entries in Google Books as well.
- www.gutenberg.org – the Gutenberg Project has scanned in some 22,000 books, all of which are available online for free.
- www.archive.org – the Open Library combines a selection of ebooks with bibliographical details of many others.

I have indicated in the text which books are available in this way.

The British Library Public Catalogue (http://blpc.bl.uk) will supply you with details of virtually every book ever published in Britain. Otherwise, talk to your local library staff to see what they can find for you. Don't forget you can borrow most books through the inter-library loan service for a few pounds.

The Internet

An increasing amount of information is available online: indeed it is now almost impossible to do family history without web access. I have assumed that readers have the Internet at home or at work, but if you haven't almost every library has computers linked to the web and there is often training available to get you started. Website addresses (URLs) were accurate at time of going to press, but if you find any links that are broken you should be able to find the answer (and any related sites) by using a search engine such as Google (www.google.com).

You will find addresses of websites scattered through the book. Apart from official sites I have included unofficial ones which I feel are serious and reasonably accurate.

There are a number of sites that offer basic information to help you research your naval ancestors, although they are not always as up-to-date as they might be. One of the best is provided by Len Barnett at www.barnettmaritime.co.uk/mainaval.htm. It is particularly good at explaining the complicated structure of the Navy which led to a huge number of different branches and ranks. The National Archives, Imperial War Museum, National Maritime Museum and Royal Naval Museum websites all have downloadable leaflets about their holdings and how to research naval ancestry. Of these TNA's is probably the most useful. Links to many naval history websites can be found at www.cyndislist.com/miluk.htm.

Websites may not be much help in providing answers to particular problems once you start researching an individual soldier. An alternative is the various online discussion forums which are ideal places to ask questions or learn from the experience of others. I belong, for example, to a First World War mailing list which has a constant stream of requests for help with members' research and these are patiently answered by other list members. In addition, there are snippets of news and debates on various related topics.

The best list of mailing lists is on the Genealogy Resources on the Internet site, which has a page devoted to wars and naval matters at www.rootsweb.com/~jfuller/gen_mail_wars.html. For details of those specifically relevant to the British Isles, visit www.genuki.org.uk/indexes/MailingLists.html. Indeed, this site lists almost all genealogical mailing lists.

There are also lists for naval history rather than naval genealogy which may be of help in understanding historical or regimental background. Yahoo Groups also has a relevant mailing list, and British Genealogy has a number of historical forums for specific wars and periods of naval history, all listed at www.british-genealogy.com/forums.

Commercial Data Providers

If you have been researching your family history for a while you will almost certainly have come across the commercial websites that allow you to have access to the census and an increasing range of other records for a fee. You can either subscribe with unlimited access to a site for a year or buy vouchers to allow access to a certain number of documents.

Unfortunately, at the time of writing, they have very little of direct interest for anybody researching naval ancestors, although new material is being added all the time. However, they all offer:

- Indexes to the births, marriages and deaths of service personnel registered with the General Register Office (see Chapter 2).
- The censuses between 1841 and 1911 (with the exception of Family relatives) (see Chapter 2).

In addition, they have the following specific naval material:

Ancestry (www.ancestry.co.uk)
- Commissioned Sea Officers of the Royal Navy, 1660–1815.
- Medal rolls.
- Royal Naval Division Casualties of the Great War, 1914–24 (also on Findmypast).
- British Naval Biographical Dictionary, 1849.

Findmypast (www.findmypast.co.uk)
- Naval casualties, 1914–19.
- Royal Naval Division Casualties of the Great War, 1914–24 (also on Ancestry).
- Royal Marines medal roll, 1914–20.

Familyrelatives (www.familyrelatives.com)
- A selection of *Navy Lists*, 1847–1952.

TheGenealogist (www.thegenealogist.co.uk)
- A selection of *Navy Lists*, 1822–1944.
- Royal Greenwich Hospital baptisms, marriages and deaths (incomplete).

In addition there are three more specialist commercial sites:

- **DocumentsOnline (www.nationalarchives.gov.uk/documentsonline)**, which has many naval resources (see below).
- **Military Genealogy (www.military-genealogy.com)**, which has a database of First World War naval casualties.
- **ScotlandsPeople (www.scotlandspeople.gov.uk)**, which has registers of births, marriages and deaths of Scottish service personnel that were sent to the General Register Office for Scotland, as well as a complete set of Scottish census records between 1841 and 1911.

Where the Records Are

Eventually you will have to use original archive material, which may prove to be time-consuming but is deeply addictive and rewarding.

Almost all naval records are held at national repositories such as TNA (formerly the Public Record Office), or service museums such as the Royal Naval Museum and, for the twentieth century, the Imperial War Museum.

Local record offices and local studies libraries may also have files relating to the Royal Navy Reserve or the papers of former naval personnel. The National Register of Archives (www. nationalarchives. gov.uk/nra) lists many holdings at local record offices, some museums and specialist repositories. An easier to use alternative is the Access to Archives database (www.nationalarchives.gov.uk/a2a). Neither is complete, however, and neither specialises in naval subjects.

The National Archives (TNA)

You will need to use TNA at some stage during the research for your naval ancestors. Most of the major sources are online through the DocumentsOnline service (see below) so you may not have to visit Kew in person. But you may want to:

TNA houses almost all the naval records you will use in your research. (Simon Fowler)

- Consult the *Navy Lists* (see Chapter 3).
- Use service and related records which are not yet on DocumentsOnline.
- Extend your research to look at the campaigns and actions in which your ancestors fought.

Researching at the archives is free and you do not have to make an appointment. Full details are available on TNA's website at www.national archives.gov.uk (click on 'About Us'). However, there are several points worth stressing:

- You will need to obtain a reader's ticket (also free) to consult original documents rather than items in microfilm or digitised form. So it is a good idea to bring two forms of identity with you on your first visit (one proving your identity, such as a passport or driving licence, the other proving your address, such as a bank statement or utility bill).

- TNA is open Tuesdays and Thursdays, 9am–7pm, Wednesdays, Fridays and Saturdays, 9am–5pm. It is closed on Sundays, Mondays, public holidays and Saturdays before public holidays.
- Although the staff are helpful and the place is thoughtfully laid out, please allow plenty of time to familiarise yourself with what is available and where it is to be found. There is much helpful information on TNA's website. At the time of writing there is a daily orientation session lasting about half an hour at 11.30am which is probably worth joining.

If you can't visit you might consider hiring a professional researcher to do the work for you. TNA website includes a list of people who specialise in naval records (or approach members of the Association of Genealogists and Researchers in Archives via www.agra.org.uk). Expect to pay between £20 and £25 per hour for this service.

TNA's Website

One of the best features of TNA is the website – www.national archives.gov.uk. It is one to which you are going to return to time and again because it has a huge number of resources.

(Crown Copyright The National Archives)

Basic navigation is simple. You can return to the homepage at any time by clicking on TNA logo on the top left-hand corner of each page. Also on each page are the four basic sections or tabs, which link to all the services and databases. In practice, you are most likely to use just two: 'About Us', which explains what TNA is and how and when to visit Kew, and 'Records', where you can find the various catalogues and guides providing background advice about the records. Indeed, just click on the big 'Records' box and this will take you to the 'Records' menu. Also on the homepage is a series of 'Quick Links' to the some of the most popular pages.

If you want to get more from the site and TNA as a whole, then concentrate on the 'Records' section as it contains guides to getting the best from the records. There are links to various pages with background information on researching family, house, local and military history; how to handle documents properly (which is important as all the records are unique and irreplaceable); and employing professional researchers if you are unable to visit Kew.

You now have the choice of going straight to the catalogue (see below) or DocumentsOnline or, if you are not sure where to start, click on one of the boxes for further assistance. You are, more than likely, going to need help finding a person. So, click on the box called 'Finding a Person'. You are then presented with lots of options. You may need to scroll down the page to you find the one that best meets your needs.

Click on it. And you are presented with a well-laid out introduction. Each one of these 'Research Signposts' (and there are nearly 150 of them) provides brief descriptions of the records, what you might expect to find and where else you might go to. There are also links to particular series (collections) in the catalogue and, where appropriate, non-TNA sources. There are also links to the In-depth Research Guides which cover the subject in a great deal more detail. Again, there are several hundred guides offering comprehensive introductions to a wide variety of subjects, including half a dozen on the Royal Navy. There are also links to the guides from the 'Records' homepage and from TNA's catalogue to its records.

Back on the 'Records' homepage click on the 'Quick Animated Guides' button. This will take you to a number of short videos explaining what archives are and how to use TNA in particular. These are surprisingly informative and are well worth viewing even if you fancy yourself as an expert!

(Crown Copyright The National Archives)

TNA's Online Catalogue

Another important section is 'Catalogues and Online Records' which has links to TNA's online catalogue, other online resources on partner websites and databases including the Trafalgar Ancestors Database, which has details of all the seamen who served with Nelson at the Battle of Trafalgar in October 1805.

(Crown Copyright The National Archives)

With nearly 11 million entries, the catalogue is the heart of the website and almost certainly its most important feature. If you are planning to do much research using records from TNA, you will need to become familiar with it.

The catalogue has various facilities that can provide additional background information. But most users will be satisfied with the basic search facility, which is the screen you arrive at after you click 'Search the catalogue'. You need to put the subject you are researching into it and can restrict searches in several ways: by date and/or by government departmental lettercode (ADM for Admiralty) or even by series (ADM 188 for Royal Navy Registers of Seamen's Services).

However, you do need to think carefully about what you are searching for – too general a search may turn up thousands of entries, too restricted, nothing at all. In part, this is because the quality of the indexing varies greatly. The search engine can only search catalogue entries and of course cannot know what you are really looking for.

You also need to be aware that useful records may appear under headings other than the one you may initially think of. Most records relating to the D-Day landings, for example, are likely to be referred to by their operational names, as this was how they were named at the time: particularly Operation OVERLORD (for the landings) or Operation NEPTUNE (for the naval preparations).

There are other ways of using the catalogue's resources. You can, for example, browse individual series of records instead of using the search engine. This is particularly useful if you are not quite sure what you are looking for, but have an idea where it should be.

Begin by clicking on 'Browse' on the top right-hand side of the screen. If, for example, you know what you are looking for was created by the Admiralty (ADM), click on the letters ADM to the left of the screen. You are then presented with an alphabetical list of series from Admiralty correspondence in ADM 1 to ADM 359, unbound outward letters sent by the Navy Board.

For information about series ADM 1, click on the underlined words in the middle column – this can be quite useful for providing context about the records and suggesting related sources (such as indexes) which may provide additional or related information. If you click on the symbol in the left-hand column, you are taken to the series list which is arranged in piece-number order.

If you already know the piece number of an item (for example, ADM 188/323), you can type it into the box on the top left of the main catalogue screen – this will take you to its description and you can also find out its context. This can be useful if you are checking up on somebody else's research or want to know more about an individual record and how it was created.

As this book went to print TNA launched a radically different catalogue called Discovery. However, the version of the catalogue described here will continue in use for some time.

DocumentsOnline (www.nationalarchives.gov.uk/documentsonline)

DocumentsOnline is the service provided by TNA to allow users to download digital copies of files and papers from the Archives' holdings. Unlike other commercial data providers (like Ancestry and Findmypast), you only pay for each document you download, rather than subscribe for a period, which is very useful if you only want one or two items. Indeed, much material is actually free, although not much of it is of immediate interest to family historians researching their naval ancestry. At present charges are £3.50 per item, £2 for medal index cards.

You can find DocumentsOnline on TNA website, although there is no link on the homepage. Instead, there is one from the 'Records' menu (click on the link at the top of the page), although it may be easier to bookmark the rather long URL.

Virtually all of the material available can only be found on Documents Online. In particular, it is very useful if you are tracing sailors, women who served in the services or are looking for wills before 1858. At the time of writing the following major series of records are available:

- First World War medal index cards (Army, RAF and merchant seamen).
- Records for women's services, 1917–19, including the Women's Royal Naval Service.
- Naval service records, c. 1756–1966 (all ranks).
- Royal Marine service records, 1842–1936 (other ranks only).
- Medals issued to merchant seamen, 1939–45.
- RAF officer service records, 1918–c. 1920 (including Naval officers who transferred when the Royal Naval Air Service became part of the RAF on 1 April 1918).
- Wills proved at the Prerogative Court of Canterbury, c. 1384–1858.

DocumentsOnline is arranged in a radically different way to other commercial sites. You can only pay for items you download by credit card. The following is a guide to using the site effectively:

1. Homepage

(Crown Copyright The National Archives)

You can only get to DocumentsOnline through TNA's homepage and then the 'Records' menu. This is the DocumentsOnline homepage. You can search either by individual collection or across the whole collection. If you choose to do the latter you must enter the name of the individual you are researching into double speech marks, i.e. "Paul Belcher". If you do not, it you will come up with every occurrence of Paul and Belcher, which of course is not very useful.

(Crown Copyright The National Archives)

2. Results

(Crown Copyright The National Archives)

I did a general search for Paul Belcher, but if you have a common name or know exactly what you are looking for it is probably easier to click on 'Wills', or whatever, and follow the same steps from there. There are three results, two wills and a medal index card which I know is definitely for my grandfather, Paul Belcher Fowler, who was an officer in the Merchant Marine during the First World War. But I am more interested in the wills.

(Crown Copyright The National Archives)

3. I click on 'Wills'. Up comes brief descriptions of the wills which provides a reasonable amount of information about each testator. I'm not sure about the clergyman, but I suspect that the sailor is 'one of mine'.

(Crown Copyright The National Archives)

4. The next screen lets you decide whether to add the will to your shopping basket. You can also add additional items to the shopping basket, so I could have all three Paul Belcher related items should I so choose. If you decide to buy the will you will need to type in your credit or debit card at the appropriate place. Once the card has been accepted you are sent a link to the document, which comes as a PDF.

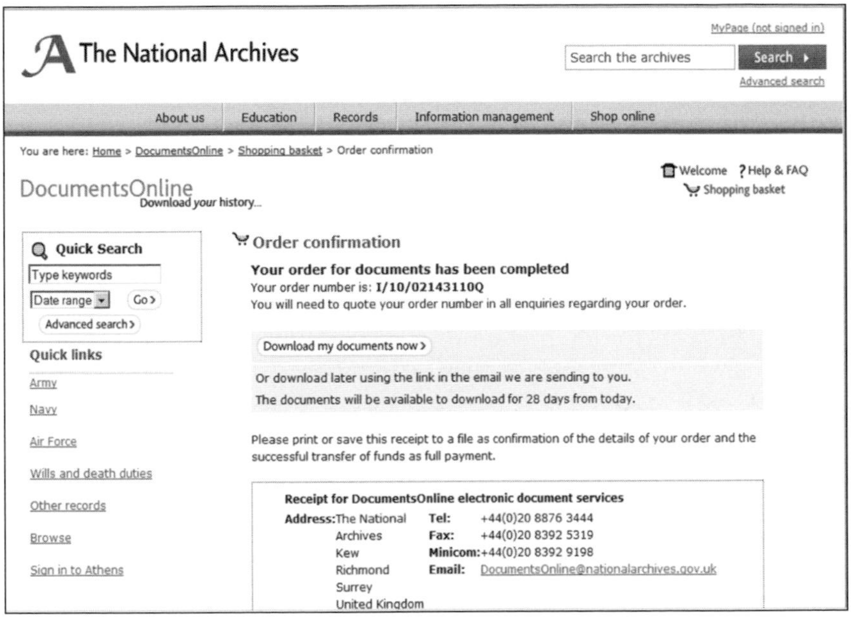

(Crown Copyright The National Archives)

5. You will need to scroll down the page to you get to the entry you want. The link is valid for twenty-eight days, so it is a good idea to save the document to your computer as soon as possible.

Family History Centres

The Church of Jesus Christ of Latter-day Saints (better known as the LDS Church or Mormons) maintain a network of family history centres worldwide, of which nearly fifty are in the British Isles. They are branches of the world's largest genealogical library, the Family History Library in Salt Lake City. These centres can provide basic help with your research and can order almost anything from the Library, which has a small and rather patchy collection of material on the Royal Navy and naval ancestors.

The Library's catalogue, together with details of family history centres, can be found at www.familysearch.org. Unfortunately, as this section was being written a new version of the website was launched which seems to have got rid of this very useful information, although there is now an excellent genealogical wiki (with some interesting pages on the Royal Navy) which is some recompense. However, there is a link at the bottom of the homepage which will take you to the site as it was originally. It is hoped that by the time this book is published matters will have improved. The London Family History Centre, the largest outside North America, has an excellent website at www.londonfhc.org, which also gives addresses of British and Irish centres.

Undertaking Research

Visiting archives for the first time can be a daunting experience, partly because they are all arranged differently but mainly because everybody also appears to know what they are doing. However, almost without exception, they are extremely welcoming and are used to receiving novice visitors.

If you intend to visit a service museum library you must ring before hand to book a seat – as they generally have very cramped reading areas. They should also be able to give you a rough idea whether they have the records you are interested in; indeed, they may have something ready when you arrive. This is particular the case with the National Maritime Museum, the archive and library of which is being extensively rebuilt until late 2011 (details at www.nmm.ac.uk/researchers/library/visiting). They can also tell you whether they allow the use of laptop computers, digital cameras and other gadgets.

You should take with you a notebook, several pencils (as pens are rarely allowed into reading rooms), your notes and change for a locker for your bag and coat (should they be provided). It is a good idea to allow plenty of time to familiarise yourself with the archive and its finding aids, particularly if you are going to make several visits. You may also want to talk through what you hope to find with the archivist or librarian on duty, as they may be able to suggest places to look and shortcuts to take.

The main entrance to the National Maritime Museum in Greenwich, home to many important collections of naval archives and artefacts. (National Maritime Museum)

Many archives now allow you to take a digital camera to take shots of pages from documents, photographs and maps. This can save both time in making notes and cost in ordering photocopies. As each archive has its own rules, you need to ask before getting your camera out. However, there is no such problem at TNA where users can snap away happily provided the results are only for their own research.

Written sources are the basis of all historical research. Using them properly makes the best use of your time and ensures that you get all you can from the records. You should:

- Note down all the references of the documents you consult, together with their descriptions, even for those items that were useless. You may need to use them again; having the references can cut the work in half.
- Read each document thoroughly, especially if you are unfamiliar with the type of record. See whether there is an index at the front or back which might help you find your man.
- Many records come in similar form. Muster books or ships' logs, for example, don't change much over time. Once you have mastered the style they are easy to go through.

- There may be an index or other finding aid. This may not always be obvious, so you may wish to ask the staff.
- If you are not sure about how to use a document, ask the staff. They are there to help!

Making Use of Your Research

Although browsing the records is a deeply satisfying (and very addictive) pastime in itself, you might want to write up your research and publish it in some way, so that other people can make use of your work (think how you benefited from the research of others) and admire your cleverness!

You may be able to persuade a local or naval history society to publish your work, or alternatively you can either publish the book yourself or approach a publisher to do it for you. What ever you do, you are unlikely to make much of a profit.

But why not submit an article about a naval ancestor and how you tracked him down to a local family history society journal. Editors usually welcome well-written, interesting contributions. But don't make it too long – it should be no more 1,000–2000 words in length.

Putting your research on the Internet is a popular alternative. Most Internet service providers (ISPs) will display your web pages for free. It is surprisingly easy to do – even for technical novices – and there are a number of books and magazines that will point you in the right direction. As you will see if you visit some of the places mentioned in this book, there are some excellent and really informative sites available. A less complicated alternative is to write a blog – basically an online diary about your researches or about the ancestors you are researching. And for those readers who have grasped what social networking is all about, you can Twitter your findings or use Facebook to spread the word.

Chapter 2

BASIC GENEALOGICAL RESOURCES

A gun crew on HMS Pelorus *during her tour of the Atlantic in 1906.* (E. Highams, *Across a Continent in a Man of War* (Westminster Press, 1909))

It is easy to overlook the basic genealogical sources of birth, marriage and death records, census returns and wills when researching sailors, but they are well worth checking out. And of course many researchers first become aware of having naval ancestors from an entry in the census or on a marriage certificate.

Most of these records are now online. Often the index can be searched for free, but you have to pay a small amount to download the information relating to an individual. One downside is that the indexing, particularly of the censuses, is not always accurate, but with a bit of imagination and perseverance you should be able to track down your man. The problem often lies in the spelling of the individual's name, which may have been wrongly written down in the first place or has been misread by the transcriber. If you spot an error, it is helpful to report it, and all the commercial websites make it easy to do this.

The major commercial data providers are Ancestry (www.ancestry. co.uk) and Findmypast (www.findmypast.co.uk). Also important is TheGenealogist (www.thegenealogist.co.uk) and to a much lesser extent Familyrelatives (www.familyrelatives.com). In Scotland the main source is Scotland's People (www.scotlandspeople.gov.uk). There isn't an equivalent for Ireland. There is really no one clear winner either in cost or customer service and as none of them, at time of writing, have any major collections of naval material, which one you choose may depend on what other resources they offer. Look out for special offers. In particular, Ancestry and Findmypast often offer fourteen days of free access for new subscribers.

Birth, Marriage and Death Records

This section relates to civilian sources. The major resources for deaths in the wars of the twentieth century are described in Chapter 5 below.

National registration began in England and Wales on 1 July 1837. In Scotland this was 1 January 1855 and Ireland 1 January 1864. The system has remained largely unchanged since then.

Unless your ancestor came from Scotland you will need to order a certificate by using indexes and noting down a reference number which you quote when ordering a certificate. At the time of writing, certificates in England and Wales cost £9.50 each (€10 in the Republic of Ireland, £6 Northern Ireland). Although the information contained naturally varies depending on the event, they all have occupations columns for new fathers, grooms and the deceased which reveal whether they were sailors or veterans.

The commercial data providers (see above) all offer indexes to English and Welsh certificates. There is a free alternative at www.freebmd. org.uk, although it is not yet 100 per cent complete.

You can order certificates online or by telephone, and both the Irish registry offices maintain reading rooms. The various GRO websites have more information:

- www.gro.gov.uk – England and Wales.
- www.nidirect.gov.uk/gro – Northern Ireland.
- www.groireland.ie – Republic of Ireland.

The Scots do things differently. There are no indexes and the certificates over 50 years (75 years marriage, 100 years births) and these are available online at www.scolandspeople.gov.uk or can be consulted at the Scotland's People Centre in Edinburgh. Fees are payable in both cases, but the good news is that they are more informative than their equivalents elsewhere in the British Isles.

Before 1837 (and indeed they are still kept today) baptisms, marriages and burials are recorded in a somewhat haphazard way by local clergymen in parish registers. Until 1812 men were not required to give their occupation, although occasionally earlier registers may indicate whether a man was a sailor. The International Genealogical Index (IGI) is an incomplete nationwide index to births and marriages. It is online at www.familysearch.org (with more resources at http://pilot.familysearch.org). Many archives and libraries have copies on microfiche. The equivalent for burials is the National Burial Index – some entries can be found at www.findmypast.co.uk, and libraries and archives may have copies on CD. Both indexes end roughly in 1837 with the introduction of civil registration.

Ancestry has many parish registers for London, while Findmypast seems to be concentrating on registers outside the capital. Scottish and Irish equivalents are much less informative or complete.

Records at General Register Offices

Each of the General Register Offices for the separate parts of the British Isles have small collections of birth, marriage and death records for service personnel including seamen. Of these the GRO in London is the most important as all information was sent here to be passed on to Scottish and Irish offices as appropriate. If you can't find Irish or Scottish sailors in the appropriate place in Dublin or Edinburgh then it is worth checking here. There are several series:

- Chaplains' Returns between 1796 and 1880 record births, baptisms, marriages, and deaths of service personnel and their families. They are generally for Army stations abroad. There is a similar series of registers between 1761 and 1924 for births, baptisms, marriages, deaths and burials of sailors and their families at home and abroad.

- Indexes to deaths in the two world wars and the Boer War. They can be useful if you do not know the service number or the ship a man was on at the time of his death, because these details are given in the registers.

These indexes are now all online, available through the commercial data providers.

The General Register Office for Scotland has in its 'minor records' series registers for the South African War (1899–1902) recording the deaths of Scottish sailors; for the First World War there are records of deaths of Scots serving as ordinary sailors (but not officers). And for the Second World War, there are incomplete returns of the deaths of Scottish members of the Armed Forces. These records are available through ScotlandsPeople.

The General Register Office of Ireland in Dublin has similar indexes and records for Irish sailors up until 21 December 1921. Later records for sailors from the Six Counties can be found at the Northern Irish GRO in Belfast. Neither records or indexes are online.

Records at The National Archives

There are several sources for birth, marriage and death records at TNA, including records for the Royal Hospital Greenwich (ADM 80) and chapels in a few Navy bases, including Malta (ADM 305), Portsmouth/Haslar (ADM 304), Chatham and Sheerness (ADM 183) and Plymouth (ADM 184). Of particular interest are the records of the Chaplain of the Fleet in ADM 338 which begin in 1845 and continue to the 1990s.

Most records of the Royal Hospital are in fact in series RG 8 (which are online at www.thegenealogist.co.uk), but otherwise you will need to use the originals at Kew. An index to marriages between 1806 and 1866 in pieces ADM 13/70-71 is available through TNA's catalogue. There is a guide to the records with the exact TNA reference at http://website.lineone.net/~mcgoa/g-contents.html.

Until 1829 officers had to prove that they were members of the Church of England as only Anglicans could reach the higher ranks in the Navy. In addition, baptismal certificates might have to be submitted as proof of eligibility for a particular entitlement, such as a widow's pension. As a

Entries from the burial register for the Royal Hospital Greenwich between 1842 and 1852. (The Genealogist / TNA RG 8/16)

result, there are several small collections of baptismal and related certificates in ADM 29 and elsewhere.

Census Returns

The first census was held in 1801 (in Ireland this was 1821), but the first one that recorded details of individuals was not until 1841. More informative, however, are those between 1851 and 1911.

Census records tell you who was living at a particular address on census night with their full name and details of their relationship to the head of household, age, occupation and place of birth. They can be useful for tracking down sailors' families or perhaps finding out a little more about the colleagues a man served with.

All the censuses for England and Wales between 1841 and 1911 are now available online at Ancestry, Findmypast and TheGenealogist for a fee. The 1881 census can searched for free at www.familysearch.org.

There are also special series of returns for Royal Navy ships. No returns are known to have survived from 1841 and 1851. However, from 1861, ships' companies were listed in special naval schedules in the

List of Officers, Crew, and Royal Marines on Board at midnight on Sunday, April 2nd, 1911.

The entry for Ernest Highams (line twelve) in the 1911 census. (Findmypast/The National Archives)

census, recording servicemen and any passengers. Vessels were enumerated in home and foreign waters. The schedules note the name, rank or rating, marital status, age and birthplace of each officer or rating, as well as location at the time of the census. In the later schedules of 1891 and 1901 name, relation to vessel (whether a member of the crew, etc.), marital status, age last birthday, occupation, birthplace and 'whether blind, deaf or dumb' were noted, along with the location. They can be found with the other census records online.

An index to ships in the 1881 census is at www.angelfire.com/de/ BobSanders/81Intro.html and for 1901 at http://homepage.ntlworld.com/ jeffery.knaggs/RNShips.html. TNA also has microfiche indexes for 1861 and indexes for 1871 and 1901 are available on CD at www.genealogy supplies.co.uk, but you really do not need them as the online indexes are fine (choose 'Royal Navy' or 'Royal Navy at Sea' for county in the search box).

The 1911 census is available through Findmypast, Ancestry and TheGenealogist. In 1911, particular care was taken to record military personnel overseas: they include around 36,000 naval personnel on 147 Royal Navy ships. You can search by name and ship. However, men on shore leave in the British Isles will be recorded where they were staying on census night and not necessarily on board their ship.

Scottish census records (1841–1911) are online at www.scotlandspeople. gov.uk. With the exception of 1901 and 1911 (now at www.census. nationalarchives.ie), Irish census records have largely been destroyed. Both are almost identical in format to those for England and Wales.

Wills

It was natural for sailors of all ranks to make wills before going on voyages, or even before going into action, because it was always uncertain whether they would return. There are several series of wills at TNA. And of course many wills were proved in ecclesiastical or civil courts.

ADM 48 contains some 20,000 wills made by warrant officers and ordinary seamen between 1786 and 1882. They normally give the testator's name (that is the name of the person making the will), rank and ship, the details of his effects and the beneficiary or beneficiaries. The wills are now all online at DocumentsOnline. In addition, there are several small series of probate records in PMG 50 and PMG 51 and several volumes of wills made by pensioners at Greenwich are scattered through the records. Pappalardo has the details. Details of naval wills in the twentieth century may be found in the papers of the Inspectors of Seamen's Wills which are at the National Maritime Museum and go up to the 1970s.

Before 1858 wills were proved in a bewildering variety of ecclesiastical courts; the most important of which was the Prerogative Court of Canterbury (PCC) in London. PCC wills are all indexed and available online at www.nationalarchives.gov.uk/documentsonline, so they are easy to check, particularly as you can search by occupation as well as name. Sailors of all ranks had their wills proved here, particularly during the eighteenth and nineteenth centuries, such as Paul Belcher, a seaman on board HMS *Milford* in 1767. At the time of writing it costs £3.50 to download a will.

Origins.net have set up a National Wills Index to collect together records from all the other myriad probate courts (www.national willsindex.com). They also have records of the Prerogative Court of York which was the second most important probate court in the country.

In 1858 a system similar to the registration of births, marriages and deaths was set up with a network of district probate registries feeding in wills to the Principle Probate Registry in London.

Calendars (or registers) are provided for each year. They list all wills proved and give a reference number which you quote if you decide to

In the Name of God Amen

I Richard Crozier Able Seaman N° 60 on the Book of His Majesty's Bomb Vessel Hecla Jo.ᵗ Ouston Esq.; &.ᵗ being of Sound and disposing Mind and Memory, do hereby make this my last Will and Testament: First and Principally I commend my Soul into the Hands of Almighty God hoping for Remission of all my Sins through the Merits of JESUS CHRIST my blessed Saviour and Redeemer and my Body to the Earth or Sea, as it shall please God. And as for such Worldly Estate, and Effects, which I shall be possessed of or intitled unto at the Time of my Decease, I give and bequeath the same as followeth that is to say I Give and bequeath unto my Wife Jane Crozier, N° 47 Great Hermitage Street Wapping London all such Wages Sum and Sums of Money as now is, or hereafter shall be due to me for my Service or otherwise on Board the said Ship or any other Ship or Vessel.

And do hereby nominate constitute and appoint the said Jane Crozier Executrix of this my last Will and Testament. And I do give and bequeath unto my said Executrix all the Rest and Residue of my Estate whatsoever both Real and Personal hereby revoking and making void all other and former Wills by me heretofore made, And do declare this to be my last Will and Testament In Witness whereof I have hereunto set my Hand and seal this twenty second Day of February in the Year of our Lord One thousand seven hundred and ninety eight and in the thirty eighth Year of the Reign of our Sovereign Lord George the 3.ᵈ by the Grace of God of Great Britain France and Ireland King Defender of the Faith &c

Signed, Sealed, Published and Declared by the said Richard Crozier as and for his last Will and Testament in the Presence of us who have hereunto subscribed our Names, as Witnesses in the Presence of the said Testator

Richard Crozier

Jas Oughton

Allin... Boatswain

Wm Boden, Cap.ᵗⁿ Clerk

The will made by Able Seaman William Crozier of HMS Heclar *in 1798. He left his possessions to his wife Joan who lived, as many sailor's wives did, in Wapping. (TNA ADM 48/17)*

order a will. These registers give the date of death, value of estate and who the executors (normally a member of the family) were. They give much the same information as a death certificate does. Calendars between 1858 and 1941 (with some gaps) are available through Ancestry or on microfiche in various archives and libraries, including TNA. Copies of wills themselves cost £5 and can be ordered by post from the Postal Searches and Copies Department, York Probate Sub-Registry, 1st Floor, Castle Chambers, Clifford Street, York YO1 9RG. Unfortunately you can't (yet) order or read post-1858 wills online.

Newspapers and Journals

Newspapers can be a surprisingly useful source, particularly if you are researching officers as they may well include details of promotions, appointments to ships, medals won and obituaries. There may even be details of courts martial. The best place to look may be the newspapers published in the naval ports. In the case of Portsmouth, for example, this was the *Hampshire Advertiser* and *Hampshire Telegraph and Naval Chronicle*.

The first newspapers emerged in the first half of the eighteenth century, but really come into their own in the 1850s when the cost came down with the abolition of stamp duty. Most towns had two or three rival papers, often aligned along party lines.

shattered, and very leaky, particularly the Ca-ira.

Return of the Officers and Men killed and wounded on board the different ships of the Squadron under Vice-Admiral Hotham's Command, in an Action with the French Fleet off Genoa, the 14th of March, 1795.

Britannia, Captain Holloway.—1 Seaman killed, 18 ditto wounded.

Princess Royal, Captain Purvis.—3 Seamen killed, 7 ditto wounded, 1 Marine or Soldier wounded.

St. George, Captain Foley.—Third Lieutenant Rt. Honeyman wounded, 4 Seamen killed, 12 ditto wounded.

Windsor Castle, Captain Gore.—First Lieutenant Thomas Hawker wounded, 5 Seamen killed, 28 ditto wounded, 1 Marine or Soldier killed, 2 ditto wounded.

Captain, Captain Reeve.—Mr. William Hunter (Master) and First Lieutenant Wilson Rathbone, wounded, 3 Seamen killed, 17 ditto wounded.

Fortitude, Captain Young.—1 Seaman killed, 4 ditto wounded.

Illustrious, Captain Frederick.—Mr. Samuel Moore (Midshipman) wounded, 15 Seamen killed, 65 ditto wounded, 5 Marines or Soldiers killed, 1 ditto wounded.

Egmont, Captain Sutton.—7 Seamen killed, 25 ditto wounded.

A cutting from the London Courier *of 8 April 1795 listing men killed in a naval action with the French off Genoa.* (British Library)

The British Newspaper Library at Colindale in North London holds the national collection of newspapers with examples of almost every issue published in Britain, together with most magazines and journal. A catalogue showing what exactly the British Library holds is at http://tiny.cc/ypuol. The Newspaper Library is moving to Boston Spa near Leeds in 2012 and at present the British Library is engaged in a massive project to digitise and make available a selection of papers online at http://newspapers.bl.uk/blcs. At present the site contains a sample of some fifty digitised newspapers and magazines published between 1800 and 1899, including the *Hampshire Advertiser* and the *Hampshire/ Portsmouth Telegraph*.

If you are lucky and your local library subscribes, you can use it at home for free. Otherwise you have to pay for access. At the time of writing it costs £6.99 for a day's access or £9.99 for seven days. It's easy to search by name or place. You can also do a preliminary search for free which will produce short extracts containing just enough information to confirm whether the story is about your ancestor or not.

The archives of a number of Fleet Street papers are also available online. Generally, you pay for a day or week's access to all of the paper's archives:

- http://archive.guardian.co.uk – the [Manchester] *Guardian* (and *Observer*).
- http://archive.timesonline.co.uk – *The Times* (and *Sunday Times*).
- www.ukpressonline.co.uk – *Daily Mirror/Daily Express*.
- http://archive.scotsman.com – the *Scotsman*.
- http://www.irishtimes.com/search/archive.html – the *Irish Times*.

It is also worth looking out for *The Times* Digital Archive, which is a rather more primitive version of the current *The Times* online archive, although it includes exactly the same material. Many local libraries subscribe to the Archive and if you have a local library ticket you may be able to access this database at home.

There were also a number of generally short-lived magazines or journals produced specifically for the Navy. They are particularly worth checking out if you are researching officers as often they include obituaries as well as details of promotions and postings. The British Newspaper Library has sets and the libraries of the Royal Naval and National Maritime museums have runs as well. One to look out for in particular is *Fleet*, published between 1905 and 1950, which campaigned for improvements in conditions on the lower deck. The most long lived is *Navy News* which has been published since 1954. Its comprehensive website at www.navynews.co.uk is mainly about today's Navy, but there are some pages on the service's history.

London Gazette

The oldest daily paper in Britain has been published by the government since November 1665. Initially, the *London Gazette* contained news stories, including accounts of the Great Fire of London, and classified advertising. For family historians it is an important source for:

- Appointments – it prints details of the appointment and promotion of officers in the services including the Navy (including those in the reserve and auxiliary forces and sometimes dockyards as well). Information given includes full name, new rank and the ship to which the individual was appointed.
- Medals – it includes details of the award of gallantry medals to both officers and ratings (such as the Victoria Cross, George Cross, Distinguished Service Cross or Conspicuous Gallantry Medal). Occasionally, a citation is included explaining in general terms how the medal was won. The individual's full name is given, together with regiment, ship or unit, rank and where appropriate service number.
- Despatches – accounts of battles, campaigns and wars written by the commander-in-chief. They would usually include the names of those officers and ratings who the commander particularly thought worthy of mention. Until the Boer War these despatches would have printed verbatim in local newspapers as news stories. Even today a Mention in Despatches remains the lowest form of gallantry award.

The *London Gazette* has been digitised and is online at www.london-gazette.co.uk. In theory it is fully searchable but this is a bit erratic, so you may need to hunt down a set of the originals to double check. Both TNA and the British Library have sets. Despite the problems with indexing, it is a very useful resource, particularly if you are researching officers.

Private Papers

A number of officers and ratings left accounts of their experiences in the Navy in the form of letters, diaries, photographs and autobiographies. It can be difficult to track them down, but some have been published or increasingly placed online. A example is the somewhat priggish diary of Aaron Thomas, a seaman onboard HMS *Lapwing* serving in the Caribbean in 1798 and 1799, at http://scholar.library.miami.edu/thomas.

If an individual's papers have been deposited with an archive it should be possible to find where they are on the National Register of Archives at www.nationalarchives.gov.uk/nra. An alternative is the Access to Archives database www.nationalarchives.gov.uk/a2a, although it is less useful for private papers.

The largest collection of private papers for the wars of the twentieth century is held by the Imperial War Museum. The National Maritime Museum and Royal Naval Museum also have extensive collections that extend back into the eighteenth century. The Second World War Experience near Leeds has a reasonable collection for the Second World War. A catalogue to the IWM's holdings is at www.iwmcollections.org.uk, but only includes a proportion of what is actually available and the catalogue itself is not terribly easy to use.

Medals

There are three types of medal (all of which are discussed in more detail below): gallantry – awarded for bravery in the field; campaign – awarded

The medals awarded to Commander Joshua Hutchinson. From left to right: the Naval General Service Medal (with a bar showing that he was awarded it for an action on the Syrian coast), the Crimean War (another bar shows he was present at the siege of Sebastopol), French St Jean D'Acre Medal and the Turkish Crimean War Medal (see pp. 50 and 51). (Richard Taylor)

A page from the roll for the St Jean D'Acre Medal awarded to Joshua Hutchinson for service in Syria. (Ancestry/TNA ADM 171/4)

to men who served in a particular action; and long service and good conduct – awarded for completing a period of service or for consistently good behaviour.

The recipients are recorded on medal rolls. The vast majority of these rolls are at TNA in series ADM 171 covering the period between 1793 and 1972. They are available online at Ancestry. Unfortunately, the rolls are not very informative. They will confirm that an individual received a medal, give his rank, service number (where there was one) and the ship he was on when the medal was awarded. There may occasionally be other information, such as where the medal was sent to or whether a man had 'run' (that is deserted) before receiving his medal.

In his *Medals: The Researchers' Guide* (TNA, 2006), William Spencer lists a number of files in ADM 1 and other Admiralty series of records that contain information about the award of medals by the Admiralty. They tend to be about the more obscure or contentious topics and may not always include details of individual recipients.

Gallantry Medals

If you have an ancestor who was awarded a gallantry medal, this fact will be noted in the *London Gazette*. Usually just the date the medal was awarded is given, but for the Victoria Cross and some other medals you may find a citation, that is a brief account of how the medal was won. The *Gazette* is online and is fully searchable at www.london-gazette.co.uk. Unfortunately, the indexing is not particularly good so it is not unknown for the search engine to miss out names. Both TNA and the British Library have bound sets and copies may be available in large public libraries elsewhere.

There are a number of websites devoted to the winners of the Victoria and George crosses and Wikipedia contains biographies for each winner and why the medal was awarded. But for more information try www.victoriacross.org.uk (which describes where winners are buried within the British Isles) and for the George Cross and its predecessors visit www.gc-database.co.uk. Details of a surprising number of naval men can be found here.

The Conspicuous Gallantry Medal was instituted in 1854 for the Crimean War, and revived in 1874 during the Ashanti War. It was only awarded to ratings and petty officers. As well as appearing in the medal rolls, recipients are listed in the *Navy List*.

A purely naval decoration was the Distinguished Service Cross (DSC), which was instituted in 1901 by King Edward as the Conspicuous Service Cross, to recognise 'meritorious or distinguished services before the enemy performed by warrant officers, acting warrant officers, or by subordinate officers of His Majesty's Fleet'. No person could be considered for the award unless he had been mentioned in despatches. The name was changed in October 1914, when it was extended to all naval and marine officers below the rank of lieutenant-commander 'for meritorious or distinguished services which may not be sufficient to warrant the appointment of such officers to the Distinguished Service Order'. There were some 1,700 DSCs awarded during the First World War and 4,500 during the Second. It was also awarded to the town of Dunkirk in 1919 'for the gallant behaviour of its inhabitants' during the First World War.

In October 1914 the Distinguished Service Medal was introduced to reward ratings and petty officers for bravery. During the Second World War it was extended to men from the other services serving on board naval ships. Some 4,100 DSMs were issued during the First World War and 7,100 DSMs were issued to naval personnel during the Second. Again the awards are recorded in the *Gazette*, in the medal rolls.

The least important gallantry award is the Mention in Despatches (MiD). Originally these were names of individuals included in despatches sent back by commanders in the field (and printed in the *London Gazette*) whose actions were regarded as being particularly noteworthy. There is no particular medal, but since 1920 recipients have been entitled to wear a silver oak leaf. It can be hard to track men who were so mentioned, but there are occasional leads. Piece ADM 7/913, for example, has details of all recipients between 1854 and 1899.

Campaign Medals

Campaign medals were awarded for taking part in particular battles, campaigns or wars. The first such medal in the Navy was the Naval General Service Medal, which was given to men who had fought in a variety of actions between 1793 and 1840, the names of which were recorded in the rolls and on metal clasps on the medal itself. It was issued in 1849 to veterans who were still alive and includes the name of the ship the man was serving on when he won it. The closing date for applications was 1851 and relatives could only apply if the original applicant died after 1 June 1847. Curiously, applications could only be received from men and not the widows or daughters of those who had served.

In fact it was not the first campaign medal to be issued to sailors. This was the China War Medal, which was given in 1842 to men who had participated in the Opium War of 1840, which saw the seizure of Hong Kong. A variety of other medals were issued during the nineteenth century for minor wars and campaigns that the Navy had participated in: the most important of which were the Queen and King's South Africa medals issued to men who had served during the Boer War (1899–1902).

Another Naval General Service Medal was awarded between 1915 and 1962 for a total of seventeen campaigns and operations that fell short of full-scale war covering operations in some very familiar places, including the Persian Gulf, Iraq, Palestine, Malaya and the Suez Canal as awards to personnel involved with minesweeping and bomb clearance. A separate clasp was awarded for the action the individual was involved with, although only one medal was awarded in total. It was discontinued in 1962 when a single General Service Medal was introduced across all three services.

During the First World War men were entitled to at least two medals – the British War and Victory medals, provided they had had twenty-eight days' service in the Navy. If they had served in France and Flanders (for example, in the Royal Naval Division) before 22 November 1914 they were entitled to the 1914 Star or if they had been in the Navy before 31 December 1915 the 1914–15 Star. Unfortunately, the Admiralty rolls are not as informative as their Army equivalents, the Medal Index Cards. In most cases all they do is to record names, service numbers, the medals awarded and the reason for the award of the medal (usually service on ships). A list of abbreviations to be found in medals rolls is at http://tinyurl.com/2acwzxd.

Campaign medals for the Second World War are discussed in Chapter 5.

In addition, the Polar Medal was awarded for service in the Arctic between 1818 and 1855 and in 1875 and 1876. Service between these dates included the search for the North West Passage and the searches for Sir John Franklin. A revived Polar Medal was introduced for men who served in Arctic and Antarctic exploration from 1904, including Captain Scott's ill-fated expedition of 1910–12. TNA Library ha22s a copy of the Polar Medal Roll (1902–99), which includes alphabetical and chronological lists of awards, with TNA references to the main sources in ADM 1 and ADM 171 and the *London Gazette*.

Long Service and Good Conduct Medals

The Naval Long Service and Good Conduct Medal was instituted in 1830. Originally, the award for seamen was for a minimum of twenty-one years' service counting from the man's twentieth birthday. The qualifying period for the medal was reduced to fifteen years in 1885, with the standard of conduct required not falling below 'Very Good'. Although only awarded to non-commissioned officers, those who had served as ratings and were subsequently commissioned were able to apply for their Long Service Medals after fifteen years, if they had served at least twelve years in the ranks. The award of these medals is recorded on an individual's service record as well as in the medal rolls (which unfortunately only survive between 1912 and 1972).

Incidentally, badges denoting good conduct consisting of gold lace chevrons were introduced in 1849 and were worn on the left sleeve of a rating's uniform. One stripe could be worn after three years very good character, two stripes after eight years and three stripes after thirteen years (see the illustration on p. 1).

Other Medals

There are a number of commemorative medals issued to men who participated in particular state occasions. They include the Jubilee Medal 1897; the Royal Victorian Medal 1901 (for taking part in Queen Victoria's funeral); the Coronation Medals 1901 and 1911; and the Delhi Durbar Medals 1903 and 1911. Some of these are available through Ancestry. Printed rolls for the 1935 Jubilee, 1937 Coronation, 1953 Coronation and 1977 Jubilee medals are available in TNA's Library.

Further Reading

There are a number of general guides to medal research, including:

Peter Duckers, *British Military Medals, A Guide for Collectors and Family Historians* (Pen & Sword, 2009)

William Spencer, *Medals: The Researchers' Guide* (TNA, 2006). William Spencer is TNA's medal specialist and a podcast of a talk he gave on naval records can be downloaded from www.nationalarchives.gov.uk/ podcasts/royal-naval-medals-introduction.htm.

Medals Yearbook (Token Publishing, annually). Contains brief descriptions of each medal together with an estimate of their worth.

A detailed guide to military medals together with high-resolution illustrations is at www.northeastmedals.co.uk/britishguide/british_ index.htm.

In addition, there are a number of published medal rolls, some of which are just transcripts of the original rolls, while others contain more about the recipients. TNA has a good collection in its Library, as do the Royal Naval Museum and National Maritime Museum. They are listed in full in Pappalardo and Spencer. And many have either been republished or are sold by the Naval & Military Press.

If you are interested in naval medals and related ephemera then you might consider joining the Naval Historical Collectors and Research Association (contact via www.nhcra-online.org or the Secretary, 81 Mountbatten Avenue, Sandal, Wakefield WF2 6HE). There is also the Orders and Medals Research Society (www.omrs.org).

Naval Education

A certificate given to Joseph Makepeace when he left TS Conway *in April 1914.* (Richard Taylor)

Schools

During the nineteenth century there were several schools that educated the sons and daughters of naval personnel. They were the Royal Greenwich Hospital School (which offered secondary education), the Royal Naval Asylum (for young children), the Royal Naval School (a public school for sons of officers) and the Royal Naval School for the Daughters of Royal Naval and Royal Marine Officers. Many records of pupils and their parents survive and can provide an unusual insight into naval families. A short history of the various naval schools can be found at http://tinyurl.com/35xvkv. A useful article about the various naval schools is Michael Egan's 'Classroom Compass', *Ancestors* (November 2007).

Royal Greenwich Hospital School

The education of the sons of residents was one of the objectives included in the founding charter of the Hospital in 1694. In 1825, the numbers were set at 1,000, including the orphans from the Royal Naval Asylum, and 200 girls. However, in 1841, it was decided 'that the propinquity of the sexes has led to many evils', and the girls section was closed.

Initially, sons of in-pensioners (those men inside the Hospital) were provided with schooling. This was extended to sons of out-pensioners, and eventually this benefit was offered to boys whose fathers were or had been serving sailors, marines or merchant seamen. It also took in some officers' sons.

The Royal Greenwich Hospital School flourished in the nineteenth century, offering three levels of education. The youngest boys and girls received elementary schooling in the Lower School (previously the Royal Naval Asylum), which admitted children initially from the age of 5 years, later raised to 9 years old. The Upper School offered secondary education with an emphasis on the skills of seamanship, and especially navigation, preparing boys for entry to the Navy at age 15 or to become apprentices in the Merchant Marine. An estimated 10,000 boys from the school joined the Royal Navy between 1874 and 1930.

The school became known as the Royal Hospital School in 1892, and in 1933 moved to Holbrook, near Ipswich.

Series ADM 73 has extensive records of the children at the Royal Greenwich Hospital School. Particularly valuable are the application papers (ADM 73/154-389): a few of which are described in more detail in TNA catalogue. Other papers in ADM 73/390-448 include some lists and other records of female pupils. Unfortunately, few records appear to survive at Holbrook.

Royal Naval Asylum

Public concern for the children of dead sailors at the battles of Brest (1794), Cape St Vincent (1797) and Camperdown (1797) and a desire to commemorate their sacrifice led to the establishment in 1798 of a school for young children called the Royal Naval Asylum in Paddington.

After the Battle of Trafalgar, George III made the Queen's House at Greenwich available for the school. There were to be 700 boys and girls at the school, and the additional wings were built to provide further accommodation for the pupils. In 1821, the Asylum merged with the Royal Greenwich Hospital School and took care of the younger pupils.

There are some records at Kew: ADM 73/89 lists the fifty boys and eleven girls at Clarence House in 1800 and 1801, and ADM 73/391-392, 440 to 441 details the girls from 1802. Minute books of the Trustees of the Royal Naval Asylum between 1800 and 1805 are in ADM 67/278. Records of baptisms of the younger children, 1822–56, are in RG 4/1678 at Kew.

Royal Naval School

During its existence, between 1831 and 1910, about 4,000 pupils entered the school. In the early years the majority left to join the Royal Navy or the Royal Marines. Records of the School are at the Lewisham Archives Centre (199–201 Lewisham High Street, London SE13 6LG; tel: 020 8314 8501; email: local.studies@lewisham.gov.uk). They include pupil records between 1831 and 1910 and records of the Scholarship Fund between 1910 and 1965. It opened in 1833 with 152 pupils.

In 1910, 3 handsome sculptures and 2 wooden memorial tablets, recording the deaths in action from the 1840s to 1906 of 51 old boys, were moved from the school chapel to the Royal Naval College Chapel in Greenwich, where they can still be seen today.

Royal Naval School for the Daughters of Royal Naval and Royal Marine Officers

When the Royal Naval School for the Daughters of Royal Naval and Royal Marine Officers was founded in 1840, it was one of the earliest girls' public schools. Many of the fathers of the girls who were admitted were naval officers on half-pay.

After enemy bombing in September 1940, the school moved to Haslemere. It is now part of the Royal School, which retains its own archives. There is a fine run of the minute books of the governing body from 1840 onwards. There is also a volume of applications between 1842 and 1877, with details of the child and her parents.

Training Ships

The Victorians set up some thirty training ships in estuaries and ports around Britain to train young men, often from very poor backgrounds, for both the Royal and Merchant navies. Often the boys came from poorer families and broken homes and it was felt that naval discipline and three square meals a day would distract them from the temptations of criminality, masturbation and smoking. Vessels ranged from fee-paying training ships for future merchant officers, such as HMS *Worcester*, through ships for pauper boys, to reformatory ships for wayward lads, like the *Wellesley* moored on the Tyne at Newcastle and HMS *Exmouth* at Grays in Essex, which was used by London's Poor Law unions for recalcitrant young men. Conditions were rarely good and discipline was often harsh, so mutinies and riots were not unknown. But for those who survived there was work waiting for them at sea.

Initially, the ships were often former naval vessels converted so that the boys could live and train on board, but gradually they were replaced by classrooms, dormitories and other facilities on shore. The Wellesley Nautical School, for example, on Tyneside, was established in 1868 to provide shelter for local waifs and to train young men for the sea. The first ship was the former frigate HMS *Cornwall*, replaced about six years later by another wooden wall, the *Boscawen*, renamed *Wellesley*. By the early 1900s the ship was taking boys from London, Manchester and Liverpool, as well as Tyneside and Yorkshire.

Mercury was the only privately owned ship providing pre-sea training for boys for both the Royal and Merchant navies. She was founded in 1885 by Charles Hoare, whose plan was to offer free, or nearly free, schooling and nautical education to boys aged from 12, when compulsory schooling ended, to 15, the minimum age for enlistment in the Royal Navy. Initially, *Mercury* was based on the Isle of Wight but moved in 1892 to the River Hamble near Southampton. The school finally closed in 1968 and the ship has recently been restored to her former splendour as HMS *Gannet* in Chatham's Historic Dockyard.

The official boys' training centre was HMS *Ganges*, which prepared tens of thousands of boys for the Navy. The vessel was originally an old man-of-war which was converted to a school in 1865. Initially based at Falmouth, the vessel moved to Shotley, near Felixstowe, in 1899. The shore station – also known as HMS *Ganges* – was opened in 1905 and prepared thousands of young teenage men for the Navy. At its peak in 1926 there were 2,200 boys on the complement. The boys finally left in 1940 when it became a general training centre. *Ganges* finally closed in 1976.

The Records

A number of registers and other records for training ships survive generally at local record offices or with the charities that originally ran them. Old boys associations can also be invaluable.

The largest charity involved was the Marine Society, which was formed in 1756 to supply men and boys to the Royal Navy. At its peak it ran several training ships, including the *Worcester* which was moored in the Thames. Some records of these ships are with the Society's library, but the majority of records have been deposited with the National Maritime Museum. More information about the Marine Society, including a short history, can be found at www.marine-society.org.

There is an excellent illustrated summary of training ships on the Thames at www.portcities.org.uk/london. It is also worth visiting the training ship pages at www.workhouses.org.uk. In addition, Phil Carradice's *Nautical Training Ships: an illustrated history* (Amberley, 2009) tells their story in more detail. This section is largely based on James Taylor's article 'An Offshore Education', *Ancestors* (December 2009).

HMS *Exmouth*
The London Metropolitan Archives (LMA) has minute books, registers and account books. Their address is 40 Northampton Road, London EC1R 0HB; www.lma.gov.uk. Most records are to be found within the papers of the Metropolitan Asylums Board, including personal records (MAB 2512). There's also an interesting article on the LMA's website at http://tinyurl.com/6ytswgx.

HMS *Worcester*
The history is covered thoroughly at www.hms-worcester.co.uk. Registers of boys are held by the Marine Society.

HMS *Conway*
The website www.hmsconway.org provides contacts for the Conway Club as well as an images archive. It includes pages listing notable Old Conways.

HMS *Arethusa* and *Chichester*
The Shaftesbury Homes has some records (www.shaftesbury.org.uk) or write to The Chapel, Royal Victoria Patriotic Buildings, Trinity Road, London SW18 3SX.

HMS *Warspite*

Registers are held by the National Maritime Museum. The Marine Society has copies of the ship's magazine from 1911.

TS *Wellesley*

The Wellesley's archives are held by Northumberland Archives (NRO 07146), including registers 1868–1933, school logbooks 1933–91, punishment books, minute books, visitors books, magazines and journals. Northumberland Archives, Queen Elizabeth II Country Park, Ashington NE63 9YF; www.experiencewoodhorn.com/collections.

TS *Mercury*

The Mercury Old Boys' Association has an extensive website at www.tsmercury.com, which includes a useful reading list as well as a history of the establishment.

TS *Mars*

Moored at Dundee, this former screw line-of-battle ship (built 1844) was in operation between 1859 and 1929 when she was broken up. There is a website dedicated to her and the boys who trained on her at www.sonsofthemars.com.

HMS *Ganges*

Despite the size of the vessel and the number of boys and men who passed through its gates, TNA has almost nothing about the establishment, although some records are apparently at the Suffolk Record Office, Gatacre Road, Ipswich IP1 2LQ; http://tinyurl.com/28xjbjc. However, there is an active HMS *Ganges* Association with an excellent website at www.hmsgangesassoc.org. The Association also runs a small museum with large numbers of photographs and mementoes about the establishment and the boys and staff. It is housed in Victory House, Shotley Point Marina, Shotley Gate, nr Ipswich IP9 1QJ; www.hmsgangesmuseum.org.uk. Another training ship for boys was HMS *St Vincent*. A page of photographs from 1896, showing life on board, is at www.portsmouth-genealogy.com/page18.htm.

Chapter 3

OFFICERS, 1660–1914

O fficers formed the executive and managerial class on board ship, in dockyards and the Admiralty. Their social background was much broader than in the Army and it was possible for people from fairly humble backgrounds to advance to the top. Horatio Nelson, for example, was the son of a Norfolk clergyman, while in comparison the father of Arthur Wellesley, the Duke of Wellington, was an Irish peer. A survey of 1,800 officers who served in the Royal Navy between 1793 and 1815 revealed 899 were from middle-class families. Of these, many were clergymen's sons, like Nelson, attracted by growing prestige and status and the chance in wartime of coming into considerable wealth from capturing enemy ships and sharing in the resulting prize money.

It is important to remember that there are two distinct types of Royal Navy officers: commissioned officers and warrant officers. In addition,

Capt Arthur Craig and his fellow officers on HMS Pelorus, *1906.* (E. Highams, *Across a Continent in a Man of War* (Westminster Press, 1909))

there were petty officers, such as midshipmen, chaplains (until 1843) and men such as boatswain's mates, sailmakers, cooks, armourers, surgeon's mates, carpenter's mates, clerks and schoolmasters, who were the equivalent of Non-Commissioned Officers (NCOs) in the Army.

Commissioned officers included the following ranks: admirals (also known as flag officers), commodores, captains, commanders and lieutenants. They were at first appointed to a ship for particular commissions (that is voyages) and were ranked according to seniority of first appointment at that rank. Incidentally, captains were always known until at least the end of the Napoleonic Wars as 'post captains' because the title of captain was given to all officers ('commanders') who commanded ships regardless of rank. They reached this rank, or in the phraseology of the time 'took post', by virtue of their first commission to command a 'post ship', that is a sixth rate one or larger.

Two other titles used in the Georgian Navy may be mentioned here because they appear to be commissioned officers' ranks, but are not: lieutenant-commander and sub-lieutenant. 'Lieutenants-commander', or 'lieutenants in command', were the captains of men-of-war too small to be commanded by commanders. Though sometimes styled captain like other commanding officers, they were not officially regarded as being in any sense distinct from other lieutenants. And there is no connection with the rank of lieutenant-commander, which was created in 1914 by re-classifying lieutenants of eight years' seniority and above. In addition, the phrase 'sub-lieutenant' referred to midshipmen and master's mates who had passed the lieutenant's examination but had not yet been promoted. These men served as watch-keeping officers on board small vessels which had no commissioned officer except the lieutenant in command. It should not to be confused with the rank instituted in 1860.

The lowest rank was a midshipman, sometimes nicknamed a 'Middy' or 'Snotty'. By the Napoleonic Wars, a midshipman was an apprentice officer who had previously served at least three years as a volunteer, officer's servant or able seaman, and was roughly equivalent to a present-day petty officer in rank and responsibilities. After serving at least three years as a midshipman or master's mate, he was eligible to take the examination for lieutenant. Wikipedia has an informative article on midshipmen.

Seniority was vital because, unless he had influential patrons in high places, an officer was promoted on this rather than as a matter of suitability or ability. It was a simple system to operate but little merit was involved. It also meant that on occasion somebody who had not been at sea for some years might be given the command of a ship. In the middle of the Napoleonic Wars, for example, officers were taking command of ships who had been long enough ashore to have forgotten much of their seamanship. In January 1808, for example, Captain Thomas Brodie took command of the new frigate *Hyperion*. Although promoted to the rank in 1802, Brodie 'had not had his foot on board a ship since he was a lieutenant' (as one of his officers recorded), and 'was consequently "rather rum in his nauticals", as the common phrase went respecting him'. If you are interested, more information about the promotion of naval officers in the eighteenth century is contained in an excellent article by N. A. M. Rodger, 'Commissioned Officers' Careers in the Royal Navy, 1690–1815', which can be read at http://tinyurl.com/2dmjndv.

As a result, seniority lists were vital in giving exact dates when a man was promoted and many survive at TNA and in naval museum libraries.

Warrant officers were the heads of specialist technical branches of the ship's company and reported directly to the captain. For administration they reported to the different boards that governed naval affairs, such as the Navy Board, Victualing Board and Ordnance Board. Indeed, they received their 'warrant' from the Navy Board. They were usually examined professionally by a body other than the Admiralty and had usually served an apprenticeship. Warrant officers included: gunners, boatswains, carpenters (warrant shipwrights from 1918), pursers and masters.

To complicate matters, in the eighteenth century, there were in fact two branches, those in the Civil Branch who were classed as sea officers, with equal status to commissioned officers – surgeon's pursers (who were in charge of the stores and victualing) and masters (responsible for the ship's navigation) who had the right to stand on the quarterdeck, and those classed as inferior officers, like boatswains and sailmakers who kept no accounts and thus had no right to the quarterdeck. Several warrant officers were classed as standing officers: boatswains, gunners and carpenters. These men were assigned to a ship for her lifetime whether she was in commission or not, and were heavily involved in her fitting out. When the ship was in reserve (that is mothballed), they were borne on the Ordinary books of the dockyard and employed in maintenance of the ship. More about warrant officers can be found at www.hmsrichmond.org/warrant.htm.

There were changes over time as warrant officers became commissioned officers: masters from 1808; surgeons, pursers and chaplains after 1843;

and, engineers from 1847 (having been created as late as 1837) became commissioned officers.

You need to be aware of this difference in your researches as there may be separate records for commissioned and warrant officers or registers divided into sections for commissioned and warrant officers (or even by trade within lists of warrant officers). The Royal Naval Museum has an article explaining all this in more detail at: www.royalnavalmuseum.org/ info_sheets_nav_rankings.htm.

This section only offers a summary of what is available at TNA. More detailed descriptions of records can be found in Pappalardo and in the following In-depth Research Guides:

Royal Navy: Officers' Service Records
Royal Navy: Officers' Service Records, First World War 1914–1918 and Confidential Reports 1893–1943
Royal Navy: Commissioned Officers' Pay and Pension Records.

Careers

Biographical Sources for Officers

The best place to start researching is in the various series of naval biographies. They are largely for officers who served in the Navy to the mid-nineteenth century. They are of varying degrees of accuracy but may

● Home ● Loney home ● Life & career ● Documents ● Album ● Ships ● Portrait ● Uniform ● Background ●   ● Search this site ●

William Loney RN - Background

Home-Loney-Background-The Royal Navy   Browse officers in command: A - B; C - E; F - G; H - K; L - O; P - R; S - T; U - Z; ??

Henry Edward Crozier R.N.   Explanation

Date (from)	(Date to)	Personal
No personal data.		

Date	Rank
8 August 1845	Entered Navy
23 May 1854	Lieutenant
16 February 1864	Commander
1 October 1873	Retired Captain

Date from	Date to	Service
10 May 1858		Lieutenant commander in Growler, Mediterranean
1884		General manager and Secretary, Hodgson's Lifeboat Co.

Top   Browse officers in command: A - B; C - E; F - G; H - K; L - O; P - R; S - T; U - Z; ??

The entry for my ancestor Henry Edward Crozier in Peter Davies' database of mid-Victorian naval officers. (www.pdavis.nl/ShowBiog.php?id=1539)

usefully supplement entries in the *Navy List* and elsewhere. Unless indicated, sets are available on the open shelves at TNA and the Royal Naval Museum. The National Maritime Museum and specialist naval museums may also have copies. But you shouldn't need to visit because – unless indicated – the volumes have been scanned and are online at www.archives.org. Some websites are also included here.

- John Charnock, *Biographia Navalis* (6 vols, 1797). This early biography only includes officers with the rank of captain and above. There are some 2,200 often with very detailed entries. Also available as a facsimile from the Naval & Military Press.
- William R. O'Byrne, *A Naval Biographical Dictionary* (2 vols, 1849). This work gives details of 'the life and services of every living officer in Her Majesty's Navy', serving or retired by 1845 – nearly 5,000 officers in all. Generally acknowledged as the most comprehensive work of its kind, it was a considerable undertaking for one man to piece together such extensive biographies. His working notes survive at the British Library. The Dictionary is also online at Ancestry and a facsimile edition can be bought from Naval & Military Press.
- John Marshall, *Marshall's Naval Biography* (4 vols, 1823–35). Memoirs of the services of flag officers, retired captains, post-captains and commanders from the Admiralty list of sea officers. There is an index to the officers who appear in it and a brief introduction at www.agbfinebooks.com/Publications/Marshall/Right%20Frame.ht.
- James Ralfe, *Naval Biography of Great Britain* (4 vols, 1828). The various editions cover naval officers who served during the reign of George III. The four volumes are also available at http://catalog.hathitrust.org/Record/000233984.
- Clement R. Markham, *The Arctic Navy List* (1875). Lists officers who served in Arctic or Antarctic regions between 1773 and 1873. The biographical notes contain varying amounts of detail on each officer and information on the ships involved. A facsimile can be bought from Naval & Military Press. The book does not appear to be available online.
- David Syrett and R. L. Di Nardo, *The Commissioned Sea Officers of the Royal Navy, 1660–1815* (Society for Naval Research, 1994). This is an updated edition of C. G. Pitcairn Jones, *The Commissioned Sea Officers of the Royal Navy 1660–1815* (National Maritime Museum, 1979). The Museum has a copy with additional annotation. There are also earlier

less comprehensive editions: the 1954 edition is available on Ancestry and another undated edition is on Familyrelatives.

- Patrick Marione, *The Complete Navy List of the Napoleonic Wars, 1793–1815* (SEFF, 2003). This CD contains the names of more than 11,000 commissioned officers who served in the Royal Navy from 1787 to about 1817. The information comprises individual's careers, their personal lives, their parents and families, the honours and pensions they earned and much more, and extends into what they did after Napoleon was finally defeated. There is an index at www.ageofnelson. org/NavyList/index.html with details of how to buy the CD. The Society of Genealogists has a copy and other large reference libraries may have it as well.

- Arthur G. Kealy, *Chaplains of the Royal Navy 1626–1903* (Portsmouth [1905]). This very rare book lists chaplains who served on Royal Navy ships. TNA does not have a copy, but the British Library and Naval Museum Library do. This book is not online.

- Details of some 1,500 naval officers who had command of a naval ship, at some stage between 1840 and 1860 is at www.pdavis.nl/SeaOfficers. php?page=2. Information provided includes details of vessels commanded, promotions and occasionally what happened after they left the service.

- Anthony Gary Brown's list of Irish naval officers who served during the Napoleonic Wars which is at www.agbfinebooks.com/ Publications/Irish/Irish%20Web.htm, although most entries are in the form of notes rather than anything structured.

- There are likely to be entries for the more famous or infamous officers (and ratings) in the *Oxford Dictionary of National Biography* and, in the twentieth century, *Who Was Who*. These reference works are available online to members of local libraries. Your local library or the council website can tell you how to access these resources at home.

- An ambitious attempt to list everybody who served in the Royal Navy since 1660 is at www.navylist.org. In practice, however, the Naval Biographical Database is largely confined to commissioned or less senior warrant and yard officers who served before about 1800. At present there are some 20,000 names on it. You can conduct a basic search of the database for free but for details you need to contact the webmaster Chris Donnithorne, who will send you an estimate of likely costs. There is a lot of very useful information and it is well worth a try if you are researching early naval officers.

- For the twentieth century (to 1945) an incomplete database of flag officers (that is men with the rank of rear admiral and above) is at www.admirals.org.uk.

The *Navy List*

The *Navy List* is the best and easiest place to start when researching an officer's career. It has been published quarterly since 1814, although it was preceded by *Steel's Navy List* from 1782. It contains seniority lists of all commissioned officers (including marines and those in the RNR and RNVR), and from 1810 features details of RN ships, including the officers serving on each vessel. Some warrant officers are also listed including masters and surgeons. The *Navy List* will give you a basic outline of your officer's career from lieutenant onwards. Confidential editions, covering the two world wars, are in ADM 177 (these indicate where individual officers were serving, with the names of ships and establishments) and other seniority lists of officers are in ADM 118, which start as early as 1717. Although now almost forgotten, seniority lists were once vital because a man's chance of promotion depended upon seniority.

TNA, the National Maritime Museum and Royal Naval Museum have complete sets of *Navy Lists*. An increasing number have been scanned and are now appearing on the websites of commercial data providers, but at present there are no complete runs, just odd volumes. There's also a little background information about the *Lists* and how to make the best use of them at www.portsmouth-genealogy.com/page23.htm.

In addition, there were three private publications. The first was *Steel's Navy List*, which was first published in 1787 and runs up to 1814. It is not authoritative but it lists officers, ships and establishments, including officers of Sea Fencibles before 1810. Also included are miscellaneous intelligence reports, vessels captured and prize money awarded. The unofficial *New Navy List* (published between 1841 and 1856) is also well worth checking, as it gives potted biographies, often stretching back decades before 1841.

Lean's Navy List dates between 1878 and 1916. *Lean's* is worth looking out for as they provide rather more information about officers than the official *Lists*, such as birth years of individuals as well as short biographies of their service and decorations. Also included are lists of ships and establishments with serving officers. Unfortunately, TNA does not have copies, although the National Maritime Museum, Admiralty

Library and British Library do. No copies appear to be online, which is a pity. Entries in early volumes may go back to the 1830s. Take, for example, Arthur Cumming who entered the Royal Navy in 1832 as a naval cadet and rose to the rank of admiral in 1880. He retired in 1882. He took part in the Syrian Campaign of 1840 and was in command of the pinnace of HMS *Frolic* in 1843 and captured a slaver, the *Vindecora*. According to *Lean's Navy List*:

> in boarding the slaver in his boat, Lieut Cumming found himself the only Englishman on board for the bowman of the boat lost his hold of the slaver, thus leaving his officer in the critical position he so ably coped with; Lieut Cumming's promptitude and fearlessness were shown by his at once shooting the helmsman of the slaver, and seizing the wheel, he ran up in the wind, and with pistol in hand kept the Spanish crew at bay until his own boat came alongside again. (www.nmm.ac.uk/collections/explore/object.cfm?ID=AAA2568)

Details of promotions are also recorded in the *London Gazette*, online at www.londongazette.co.uk.

Service Records

Apart from the *Navy Lists*, there are three main types of record in which you may find details of an officer's service. There is some overlap between them, so it may be necessary to check more than one source.

- Registers of Officers' Service, 1756–1966 in ADM 196. During the nineteenth century the Admiralty started to keep service registers for officers in which a page was opened for recording each man's career. Early service records tend to be very basic; it is only from the late nineteenth century that details such as the officer's date and place of birth and next of kin are provided. It is also worth noting that these records are not one single collection of records, but several series of service records, so it is possible for an officer to have multiple service records.

  Most of the 170,000 entries cover the period between 1840 and 1920, with deaths entered to the 1950s. Most registers give dates and places of birth and death, home address, name of wife and date of marriage. All will give you the names of the ships on which the officer served. These registers provide the most complete and convenient source of

The entry in the Register of Officers' Service for Cdr Joshua Hutchinson, which contains brief information about the ships he served in. His medals can be seen on p. 30. (TNA ADM 196/2)

An additional service record for Commander Hutchinson describing his service in the Crimea. (TNA ADM 196/36)

information about the career of an officer. They have been digitised and are available through DocumentsOnline.

- Miscellaneous registers of officers' service in ADM 6, ADM 11 and ADM 29. These series contain a variety of registers generally for the period before the start of the registers in ADM 196. There seems little rhyme or reason to which records are where nor are there many long runs of records. In addition, some of the piece descriptions in the catalogue leave much to be desired, although there are plans to improve things.
- Most of ADM 6 consists of service records of sea, marine and naval officers and includes commission and warrant books, succession books and registers of shore appointments, as well as some service registers. There are also collections of passing certificates for lieutenants and warrant officers, returns of the 1822 survey of officers' ages and leave books.
- The records in ADM 11 include some original returns of officers' services (including surgeons, chaplains, etc.) in addition to various related entry books and compilations, together with the appointments of commissioned and warrant officers. The series also includes some registers of commissions and warrants entered by ship. Most records date between 1780 and 1847.
- ADM 29 mainly consists of service records compiled by the Navy Pay Office from ships' musters and pay books for ratings, warrant officers, and occasionally commissioned officers. In addition, there are full and half-pay registers, in support of applications made by seamen for pensions, gratuities and medals. Records date between 1802 and 1919.

A section from the three pages of scribbled notes in the register for Arthur Craig (1871–1943), who joined the Navy in 1887, eventually reached the rank of vice admiral before retiring in 1923. He commanded Pelorus *between January 1908 and April 1909.* (TNA ADM 196/123)

- Returns of Officers' Service, 1817 and 1846 in ADM 9. In 1817 and 1846 the Admiralty tried to improve its personnel records by sending out surveys for officers to complete and return, although not everybody did. An index can be found in the Open Reading Room at Kew. Other survey returns from warrant officers can be found in ADM 6 and ADM 11.

- Certificates of Service, 1802–94 in ADM 29. These records give the service of warrant officers (and ratings) who applied for a naval pension or admission to the Royal Greenwich Hospital. They give a brief record of ships and dates, and total time in paid employment.
- Full and Half Pay Registers, 1697–1924 in ADM 22–ADM 25, PMG 15. Certificates of service were compiled by the Navy Pay Office from the full or half-pay registers which can be used to assemble similar records. These registers usually give simply the name and the sum payable, but they can be used to confirm when an officer was employed or unemployed. (For more about half pay see below, p. 57.)

Officers' Passing Certificates

These certificates were issued to men who passed an examination that established their suitability for appointment to a particular rank. They often provide information about a man's service prior to the examination and sometimes have supporting papers, such as certificates of birth or baptism.

The most important series are those for lieutenants, for whom certificates were introduced in 1677 and run to 1902. Applicants were tested about whether they had the requisite skills and knowledge to become commissioned officers. Originally, the certificates were introduced to ensure that only qualified men became lieutenants rather than, as was the case in the Army, those who bought their position as a result of their social background or wealth. The aim was largely successful, although advancement might still depend on social standing and influence.

Candidates had to be at least 20 years old and have served six years at sea, with a minimum of two years' service as a midshipman. They also had to produce certificates signed by captains with whom they had served confirming their abilities.

Applicants were usually interviewed by a panel of three senior captains. Examining officers made up their own questions as none were provided by the Admiralty. Many officers, like Charles Middleton, later Lord Barham, took their examining role very conscientiously and asked candidates questions like this: 'Upon receiving orders to sail from Spithead with a south-east wind, at what time of tide will you begin to unmoor that you may take the advantage of it plying down to St Helens? … What officers will you send for, and what directions will you give them when the ship is to be unmoored?'

The lieutenant's passing certificate for Horatio Nelson. (TNA ADM 107/6)

For many candidates the examination was inevitably an ordeal. In May 1805, one young man, William Badcock, was sent forward by his captain, Thomas Fremantle of the *Neptune*, to sit his exam. He was in a state of extreme nerves and the three captains on the examining board allowed him to sit quietly for a few moments so that he would do himself justice. Then they began.

> I was desired to stand up, and consider myself on a quarterdeck of a man-of-war at Spithead – 'unmoor' – 'get underway' – 'stand out to sea' – 'make and shorten sail' – 'reef' – 'return into port' – 'unrig the foremast and bowsprit, and rig them again'. I got into a scrape after reefing for not overhauling the reef tackles when reefing the sails (because unless those tackles were overhauled, the sails would not set fair). However they passed me, and desired me to come again the next day to receive my passing certificate. I made the captains the best bow I could and, without staying, to look behind me, bolted out of the room.

The examination was often easier for candidates with influential social and political backgrounds. Nelson's uncle, Maurice Suckling, who was secretary to the Navy Board, was on the board when Nelson passed his examination in April 1777.

In is important to remember that successful candidates were not guaranteed a commission. In times of peace, in particular, it could be many years before a man received his first appointment. Most lieutenants' passing certificates date between 1691 and 1902, although there are gaps for 1677–90, 1833–53 and for those issued abroad. To complicate matters some men were promoted without having to pass an examination, generally if a vacancy occurred overseas or a man was promoted as the result of a particular act of bravery.

Certificates are likely to give a man's age, the members of the board who examined him and, from 1778, the ships he had served on before his examination.

Increasingly, copies of baptismal certificates may be found with the certificates. And from 1802 the prospective lieutenant's age and place of birth on joining the Navy is also recorded. From this date it is possible to find original certificates signed by captains confirming a prospective lieutenant had served with him. They can be found in ADM 6/86-118; ADM 13/88-101, 207-236; ADM 107/1-63. A nominal index is provided by Bruno Pappalardo's *Royal Navy Lieutenants' Passing Certificates, 1691–1902* (vols 289–90, List and Index Society, 2001). Copies of this book are in TNA library, the major maritime museum archives and many large reference libraries. There is also a useful article, Bruno Pappalardo's 'A Record of Merit', *Ancestors* (June 2002), which most of the above section is based on.

Passing certificates were also eventually introduced for warrant officers. These too can be found at Kew: Boatswains (1810–13, 1851–87) are in ADM 6 and ADM 13; Carpenters (1856–87) ADM 13; Clerks and Assistant Clerks (1852–99) ADM 13; Engineers (1863–1902) ADM 13; Gunners (1731–1812, 1856–87) ADM 6 and ADM 13; Masters (1660–1863) ADM 106, ADM 6 and ADM 13; Paymasters (1851–89) ADM 13; Pursers (1813–20) ADM 6; Surgeons (1700–1800) ADM 106. Ask the staff in the Open Reading Room for indexes to engineers' and surgeons' passing certificates.

Miscellaneous Records

Details of wives and dates of marriage are usually included in the service registers. In addition, collections of marriage certificates are held in pieces ADM 13/70-71 (these are searchable by name on the Catalogue), and in ADM 13/186-192. The certificates were submitted from 1866 to 1902. The names of officers' widows and children can often be found among the records of pensions or payments made by the Admiralty or charities listed below.

Also worth looking out for are the black books, leave books and examinations. Black books, kept by the Admiralty to record the names of officers who had disgraced themselves and who were not to be employed again, are in ADM 12/27B-27E (officers 1759–1815) and ADM 11/39 (warrant officers 1741–1814). Leave books recording leave granted to officers between 1783 and 1847 are in ADM 6/200-211. Examination results for officers attending the Royal Naval College in Greenwich (1876–1957) are in series ADM 203.

Pay and Pensions

There many sources at TNA for the payment of pay and pensions to naval officers and their widows. They often seem to duplicate each other and may appear in half a dozen different places. However, the value of these records is perhaps limited as they tend to be little more than entries in large volumes recording how much money was paid each month.

There were four principal bodies responsible for the payment of various pensions to commissioned officers:

- The Admiralty/Navy Pay Office.
- Royal Greenwich Hospital.
- The Charity for the Payment of Pensions to Widows of Sea Officers.
- The Compassionate Fund.

TNA has records of each of these bodies, although they are not complete. The responsibility for paying naval pensions was taken over by the Admiralty from these bodies during the nineteenth century, leaving only the Royal Greenwich Hospital as an independent body paying various supplementary and special pensions. From the 1850s, the Paymaster General (the records of which have the PMG lettercode) began to take over responsibility for paying pensions.

Full pay

The records are in ADM 24 for the period between 1795 and 1905. They record payments to commissioned officers who were actively employed. They normally give only the officer's name and the exact dates of each employment, but they can also be used to compile a record of an officer's successive employments.

From 1795 to 1835, there are separate indexed registers for each commissioned rank. These were replaced in the 1830s with general registers to which there are indexes. No registers survive between 1873 and 1903.

Half Pay

Except in time of war there were always too many naval officers and too few ships for them to command. Promotion depended on individuals moving up the succession lists until they reached the top and were offered a post. The solution was to put officers, for whom there were no vacancies at sea, on to half pay. Since there were no general schemes of retirement before the mid-1800s, half pay frequently operated as a type of superannuation and no test of actual fitness was applied. Thereafter, half pay declined in importance, becoming simply a means of filling short gaps in the career of serving officers. It was abolished in 1938. Half-pay records are mainly lists of names and the sums payable to them, but they sometimes include addresses and other information. In conjunction with full-pay registers, they can be used as they were originally in compiling certificates of service, to reconstruct an officer's full career. Most records are in ADM 25 but there are some in ADM 6, ADM 23 and PMG 15.

Pensions

From 1666, yard officers and some captains received superannuation or retirement pensions. The possibility of getting such a pension was extended to most senior lieutenants in 1737, to 'yellow admirals', that is captains temporarily promoted to the rank of admiral without distinction of squadron (a practice known as 'yellowing'), from 1747, and to retired captains from 1786. No officers were entitled to superannuation until 1836, when officers became eligible for superannuation either automatically or upon application on reaching a specified age and seniority. Details of pensions (1661–1781) are in ADM 18/39 and (1781–1821) ADM 22/1, 17, with other records in pieces ADM 7/809, ADM 22, ADM 23/106-107 and ADM 181/127. Records of pensions after 1836 are in PMG 15, PMG 19 and for dockyard officers PMG 24, as well as various odd volumes scattered through several ADM series.

But of course not every officer retired to live out their days on their pensions. Then as now, life in the Navy provided skills and confidence that were useful in a whole range of other professions. After the Napoleonic Wars the brave but reckless Thomas Cochrane (1775–1860) established the Chilean Navy, which played a major role in that country's struggle for independence (he is also said to be the model for many fictional naval heroes such as Jack Aubrey and Horatio Hornblower, see www.hms.org.uk/nelsonsnavycochrane.htm). Less romantically, many men joined the coastguard (see Chapter 6), but surprisingly often they entered the police, prisons and Poor Law system. John McHardy (1801–82), for example, was the first Chief Constable of Essex in 1841, having previously risen to the rank of captain in the Navy (playing a prominent part in combatting the slave trade) and then joined the coastguard as an inspector in Norfolk and the Isle of Wight. His naval training proved very useful in shaping and inspiring the new police force. Two of his sons, Hector and Wallace, also became chief constables after service in the Royal Navy.

THE EARL OF DUNDONALD.

FROM A PICTURE BY JAMES RAMSAY

London: Richard Bentley 1866.

A contemporary woodcut portrait of Thomas Cochrane, the founder of the Chilean Navy. (Simon Fowler)

Royal Greenwich Hospital Pensions

Officers were also eligible for Greenwich in-pensions, that is becoming a resident at the Hospital itself: details are in ADM 73/36 (1704–1846). From 1814, there were a small number of out-pensions to captains, commanders and lieutenants: details of which are in ADM 22/47-49, 254, ADM 165 and especially PMG 70 (1866–1928) and PMG 71 (1846–1921).

Wounds and Disability Pensions

From 1675, the Admiralty paid pensions for wounds acquired on active service to commissioned officers. These pensions could be combined with full pay, half pay or superannuation. A full list can be found in TNA's In-depth Research Guide *Royal Navy: Officers' Service Records*.

Widows' Pensions

From 1673, widows of commissioned officers killed in action were eligible for Admiralty pensions. Again you need to know roughly when the pension began to be paid and the rank of the deceased officer. These records also contain references to dependants. There are various volumes in ADM 6, ADM 7, ADM 18, ADM 22, ADM 23, as well as from 1836 in PMG 19 and PMG 20.

The Charity for the Payment of Pensions to the Widows of Sea Officers was established in 1732. It was administered by trustees but was more an official pension fund than a private charity. Its income came from parliamentary grants and a compulsory deduction of three pence in the pound from officers' wages. It paid pensions to the poor widows of all sea officers regardless of how or when they died, but not to those who were left comfortably off. In 1836 the responsibility for officers' widows' pensions was assumed by the Admiralty and the test of poverty abandoned. In addition to these pensions, a lump sum of one year's wages, known as the Royal Bounty, was payable to widows, orphaned children or mothers aged over 50 of officers, ratings and marines killed in action. Minutes (1732–1824) are in ADM 6/332-334.

Certificates and other papers submitted by applicants (1797–1829) are in ADM 6/335, and papers of cases referred to the Court of Assistants of the Charity for decisions between 1808 and 1830 are in ADM 6/385. Records relating to claims on the Royal Bounty between 1675 and 1822 are in ADM 106/3023-3028. There is an index to these records, please ask in the Open Reading Room at TNA. Later pay lists (1739–87), with details of the dead man, the applicant and the sum paid, are in ADM 106/3018.

Compassionate Fund

From 1809, the Compassionate Fund (later Compassionate List), which was voted by Parliament and administered by the Admiralty, paid grants and pensions to the orphans or other dependants of officers killed in action. Records are in ADM 6/323, ADM 22/239, 253 (1809–1932) and correspondence (1809–1845) in ADM 2/1085-1086, 1097. There are also some later registers recording the payment of compassionate allowances (1866–1932) in ADM 23, and details of payments to families on the Compassionate List (1837–1921) in ADM 23 and PMG 18.

Miscellaneous Records

From 1871 some Royal Greenwich Hospital pensions were paid to deserving officers. The money often came from special funds such as the Travers, Popeley and Canada funds. In 1837 good service pensions were created, to be paid to deserving flag officers and captains and later to civil officers of equivalent rank. They could be used to supplement full or half pay, but were forfeited on promotion. Records are in ADM 23 and PMG 16.

There are also a number of other records relating to officers' or widows' pensions, of which probably the most interesting are the applications in ADM 45 by next of kin for the unpaid wages or pensions of deceased officers, their widows or civilian employees of the Navy which date between 1830 and 1860. Some applications are supported by birth or marriage certificates or wills. There is a fully searchable index on TNA online catalogue.

Memorials

The 1805 Club (www.1805club.org) is dedicated to the memory of the officers who fought with Nelson and endeavours to restore and maintain their graves and memorials. They have published a guide to these memorials and their locations. More generally the UK National Inventory of War Memorials has records for 60,000 war memorials. The vast majority of these are, of course, for the two world wars, but their database includes many earlier memorials to naval officers.

Memorial inscriptions for a miscellaneous selection of eighteenth- and nineteenth-century officers can be found at http://glosters.tripod.com/Taf.htm. It is by no means complete, but occasionally can be useful. As was the fashion of the time, many of the inscriptions make the deceased seem almost saint-like. For example, the memorial to George Heigham in St Mary's Church in Bury St Edmunds:

> George Heigham youngest son of Pell Heigham Esqr and Penelope his wife was born Set.15.1770 and being 8th Lieutenant of his Majesty's Ship the Royal George, fell, by a cannon shot in action with the French Fleet, May 29th 1794. Such were the amiable qualities, such the professional merits of this promising young officer, that his early death will long be a subject of deep regret to his friends, and may be esteemed, no inconsiderable loss to his country.

See also p. 94 for further details on memorials.

Admiralty Digests and Indexes

Years ago when I worked in the reading rooms at TNA the staff often had to show people the Admiralty indexes. This was always an occasion. The indexes were large and very heavy volumes which had to be carefully lifted onto desks for people to consult. When it was my turn I sometimes felt that I had been taken back a couple of centuries as the finding aids and skills needed to use them had not changed much over the decades.

The records to which they refer – in-letters in ADM 1 (that is despatches, telegrams and correspondence arriving in Whitehall), out-letters in ADM 2 (that is copies of letters, etc. being sent out) and the Admiralty Board minutes (ADM 3) – are the very core of the Admiralty's history. Here are to be found correspondence with Nelson and the other great commanders, papers about courts martial or the commissioning and loss of ships, reports from dockyards and battle squadrons, alongside entreaties for employment or promotion.

These records are not easy to use. The indexes – in series ADM 12 – provide extraordinary detail, being in effect a nominal index of naval officers, warrant officers and even ratings; of marine officers; of 'persons of distinction'; and of ships (naval and merchant vessels, and foreign ships as well as British). The names of RN ships are generally shown in red ink. The names of the individuals included in the index are not just the authors of letters to the Admiralty; the index mentions people referred to in the content of letters and reports. They are most useful between 1793 and 1913.

Pappalardo describes how to use these records. In addition, there is an In-depth Research Guide which you can download from TNA website.

In fact, you may not have to use them. The correspondence to which they refer, mainly in ADM 1, are arranged by cut (or subject) and then by file from about 1913, so can be searched through the online catalogue. Before 1913 they are arranged by subject by year, so, for example, all the correspondence for 1805 with captains whose surnames beginning with the letter A are in ADM 1/1451, so you will have to order up the box and search through it hoping to find a letter from your ancestor. There a few indexes, notably for courts martial between 1680 and 1702, in the online catalogue.

From the 1840s, the habit developed of collecting together all the papers on a certain matter. These bound files, known as cases, are worth looking out for if, for example, you are researching the loss of a ship or a particular action. They are recorded in the index and digest, but most, certainly for the twentieth century, are described in the online catalogue. However, you will need to check other series, because relatively few are in ADM 1. Some very early cases are in ADM 7, but of more importance is the correspondence in ADM 116, ADM 137 (for the First World War) and ADM 199 (for the Second World War).

Chapter 4

RATINGS AND PETTY OFFICERS, 1660–1914

The vast majority of men on board a ship were of course not commissioned officers, they were ordinary sailors with various ranks and specialisms. In the Royal Navy all those who are not officers or petty officers are known as ratings (rates is a modern usage). The term is very old, being already commonplace when scales for prize money were announced in 1702. The substantive naval ranks, from the lowest to the highest, were: able seaman, leading seaman, petty officer and chief petty officer. With the rank of ordinary seaman included – a rank allocated to men in training – the Navy had a total of five ranks for ratings and non-commissioned officers. Each man had his own trade or specialism, perhaps as a sailmaker, carpenter or in the rigging, which led to a bewildering number of rankings and pay rates.

In peacetime, the Navy recruited all its men as volunteers. Many of them were boys, often helped by charities such as the Marine Society,

On board a ship at sea. (William Glasscock, *Naval Sketch Book* (1835))

which funded careers at sea for street boys in major cities (see Chapter 2). As professional sailors required years to master their craft, it was as well to start early. Boys commonly began at the age of 10 or 12, and there was plenty of work for small, nimble seafarers, both on deck and in the rigging.

By 16, most boys would be competent seamen, able to work aloft, reef sails, knot and splice ropes and steer the ship. At the same time, their bodies took on a characteristic broad-shouldered, barrel-chested physique – the result of heavy hauling and lifting and often being bent double over the yards – while the constant roll of the ship gave them a peculiar rolling gait.

Most sailors worked at sea until their mid-twenties when they left for less onerous work on shore or in the coastal traders. A small proportion remained at sea, filling vital specialist roles such as master, responsible for the navigation of the ship, carpenters and sailmakers.

Mature sailors were a valuable commodity, the pinnacle of working-class labour in the eighteenth century, better paid and better treated than any shore-bound contemporaries. Their status was most obvious in wartime, when the Navy needed three or four times as many seamen as in peacetime.

Even so, the vast majority of men were really only needed for their muscle power. Even on the state-of-the-art steam-powered warship HMS *Warrior*, which was launched in 1860, 600 of the 700 crew members spent their time lifting sails, hauling ropes, turning the capstan or manning the pumps.

On board, the sailors were divided into watches, usually two, which shared the work, and into messes of eight to ten individuals, for catering. Each mess was a self-assembled group of like-minded men, usually with the same skills and rank. They shared the domestic chores of preparing food, collecting cooked dishes and washing up. These small groups formed the core of shipboard life and were the basis of effective teamwork, working together in key areas, perhaps in the rigging or as a gun crew.

Badges and Uniforms

Men on the lower deck were not provided with uniforms until 1857, when the first Uniform Regulations for Petty Officers, Seaman and Boys were published. Officers, however, were first issued with uniforms as early as 1748, although their dress was not standardised until 1795.

However, as a result of bulk buying from slop-sellers and naval chandlers, there was some degree of uniformity for ratings before then. The style of uniforms worn varied according to the whim of individual captains, so as a man moved from one ship to another, he had to buy himself new kit. On one occasion in 1853, the commanding officer of HMS *Harlequin* paid for his boat crews to dress as harlequins, an incident that may have contributed to the Admiralty's decision to adopt a standard uniform.

The rules for ratings' uniforms were introduced to prevent abuses of this kind and to give a sense of unity across the service. Although modernised over time, the uniform is still not dissimilar to that of 150 years ago and it has been imitated by navies around the world.

But the rules did not standardise everything. In his comprehensive *Badges and Insignia of the British Armed Services*, William May noted that:

> Many men obtained their badges from private sources, so there was a great variety in cut and size, and it was not until standardised woven designs appeared in 1879 that there was real uniformity. The National Maritime Museum has a white frock from the Crimean War, which has the badge of a second class petty officer crudely worked in white thread on a piece of blue serge.

One item of attire, however, was soon standardised. Royal Navy ratings were wearing hat ribbons by the 1840s, but it was not until the first uniform regulations were published that tallies (that is the ribbon on the cap) bearing the ship's name gained official recognition. The rules did not specify how the ribbons were to be marked, so it was customary for sailors to paint on the names of their ships in large capitals. The gilt-wire lettering still familiar today was officially introduced in 1858.

As a rating was promoted he would wear the appropriate badges of his substantive rank on his left sleeve. These might be a fouled anchor for leading seaman or crossed anchors and a crown for a petty officer first class. On the right sleeve he would wear badges displaying his non-substantive ratings, that is basically his trade or specialism.

It is easy to be confused by the stripes on sailors' uniforms. These are not badges of rank, but good conduct stripes, awarded for varying periods of service during which the sailor's yearly conduct assessment did not fall below 'very good'. These badges were sought after, because they also carried extra pay. Service records show when good conduct badges were granted, if the sailors were deprived of badges and when they were restored. To see what a seaman might have looked like, see the picture on p. 1.

The loss of a badge lowered the annual assessment to 'good' – or even lower in the worst cases. This would have an impact on the award of the Long Service and Good Conduct Medal, which required a minimum number of successive years during which the man was assessed as 'very good'. Conduct badges were always worn on the left sleeve, below the badge indicating the man's substantive rating.

Also on the right sleeve would be an embroidered badge showing his trade. These began in 1860 when gunnery instructors were given embroidered badges to wear on their right sleeves. These insignia first consisted of a gun superimposed on a crossed rifle and cutlass with a crown above for instructors and a single gun with or without a crown for first or second class seamen gunners. By 1885, the introduction of the torpedo required another set of separate ratings. As a result, both torpedoes and guns might appear on badges. There were other modifications in 1890, when badges were introduced for other trades, including stokers and signallers. Just to add to the confusion, yet another reorganisation followed in 1903 and other badges were introduced later in the century. All this reflects the very many ranks and rolls that an ordinary seaman or able seaman could be (see also Appendix 1).

An introduction to the topic, with illustrations, Richard Taylor's 'First Class Boys', appeared in issue 90 of *Ancestors* (February 2010). The most comprehensive guide to the thorny subject of naval badges is W. E. May, W. Y. Carman and John Tanner, *Badges and Insignia of the British Armed Services* (Adam and Charles Black, 1974). TNA and the maritime museum libraries have copies.

If you are trying to puzzle out what the badges are on the uniform of a naval ancestor, then help may be available through the British and Commonwealth Military Badge forum at www.britishbadgeforum.com. You will need to register before posting enquiries. Many badges can be viewed online (as well as purchased) at www.kellybadge.co.uk/stock/navy.htm. Examples of badges and insignia of ranks as worn by the Royal Navy during the Second World War are at www.naval-history.net/WW2aaRN-PayTables00Ranks-Badges.htm. Indeed, this is a good introduction to the subject in general.

On the wider issue of uniforms there are useful introductions on Wikipedia and at www.seayourhistory.org.uk/content/view/640/808.

The Records

More details can of course be found in Pappalardo and in two In-depth Research Guides that can be downloaded from TNA website – *Royal Navy: Ratings' Pension Records* and *Royal Navy: Ratings*.

Men Entering Between 1667 and 1853

There are no service records for ratings before 1853 because men were discharged at the end of each voyage and could then to choose to serve in merchant vessels if they so wished. Before you start research it is

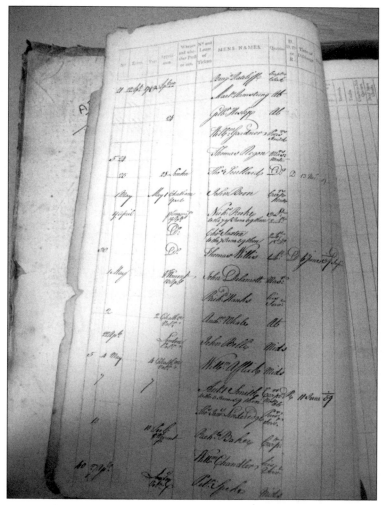

A page of the muster book for HMS Sandwich, *1760.* (TNA ADM 36/6768)

helpful to know which ship your ancestor served with. The main sources for tracing naval seamen before 1853 are:

- Muster and pay books of the individual ships (for which you need to know the name of at least one ship served on, and a rough date).
- TNA's Trafalgar Ancestors Database.
- Applications for pensions, which include certificates of service. In the early 1800s pensions were more likely to be paid to warrant officers than ordinary seamen, but after 1834 pensions, and therefore records for seamen, become more common.
- Applications for admission to Royal Greenwich Hospital as in-pensioners.

Ships' Musters and Pay Books

If you have the name of a ship and a date, it is possible to trace a seaman's service both backwards and forwards using the ships' musters in ADM 36, ADM 37, ADM 38, ADM 39, ADM 41, ADM 115 and ADM 119. They date between 1667 and 1887. The purser on each ship had to keep a record of the men on board, including their date of entry to the ship, their rating (and whether they had been pressed), the amount paid to them, clothing and tobacco issued and even at times treatment for venereal disease. From 1764, they should provide a man's age and place of birth, although this has not always been entered. The information is often vague or inaccurate but it may give clues which can be followed up in parish registers and other records. From about 1800, description books (which give age, height, complexion, scars and tattoos) may be included with musters.

Where a muster is missing you can use the ships' pay books in ADM 31, ADM 32, ADM 33, ADM 34, ADM 35 and ADM 117 to confirm that a man served on a particular ship. Until the introduction of continuous service in 1853 men often moved between naval and merchant ships which can make tracing individuals very difficult.

Each muster or pay book contains several lists. The first and by far the largest is the general one for officers and crew. There are separate lists for boys, marines and for supernumeraries, depending on whether they were being paid or only received victuals. The list of supernumeraries should not be ignored because it often includes details of men who have joined or are leaving the ship.

Even a brief flick through the record for a single vessel shows the wide variety of people in the Navy at the time. The muster for the *Foudroyant* for May 1798 (ADM 35/639) includes an entry for 31-year-old Thomas Howard from Colchester, an able seaman. He was discharged to hospital in Plymouth during the following month. James Denis from Guisborough, North Yorkshire was the same age. He received £86 18s 8d in wages and paid out 12s 8d for tobacco.

But these books are not always an ideal source because the record keeping is not always very good and sailors' names are often misspelt and the volumes themselves can be heavy and difficult to handle. The records are described in more detail in Brian Lavery's *Royal Tars* (Conway, 2010). And Pappalardo provides a list of abbreviations which you are likely to come across in these muster books.

Description Books

Description books were kept in order to identify deserters and contain physical descriptions of individuals. With so many men who were not on board of their own free will, coupled with often atrocious conditions on board, it is little wonder that desertion was a major problem until well into the nineteenth century. To prevent men from running (the naval term for desertion) it was rare to let men go ashore during a voyage, and the design of naval hospitals was as much about preventing patients from escaping as it was providing a cure.

These books are to be found either at the National Maritime Museum (which has them before about 1836) and TNA, where they can be found in series ADM 38 between 1836 and 1872. Description books are identified with the suffix D in descriptions in TNA's catalogue.

The descriptions of individual ratings are often unflattering but can be revealing about their careers at sea. Samuel Lindley, who served at Trafalgar in *Bellerophon*, was 24 years old, from Lenham in Suffolk and already had three years' experience in the merchant service. He had a pale, thin face but was considered 'well-looking'. Meanwhile, his ship mate, Isaac Harrison of Norwich, had spent 32 of his 45 years at sea. He is described as being 'bald, a little deaf, thick set and strong made' and was a quarter gunner (which may explain his deafness) (NMM LBK/38).

Again, these records are described in more detail in Brian Lavery's *Royal Tars* (Conway, 2010).

Allotment Books

A small series of records in series ADM 27 – allotment registers – may also be useful. They are being catalogued by TNA staff and it is possible to search by ship and (to a much lesser extent) name. Allotment registers record the payments made by ratings and petty officers to their families at home.

The intention of the allotment scheme, which ran between 1795 and 1852, was to improve working conditions and to make enlistment more attractive. Initially, only a small number of petty officers and ratings joined the scheme, but by the 1810s one seaman or marine in three was a member, and by the 1850s half the number of seamen and marines made contributions. Up to half of a man's pay could be allotted in this way to wives, children or parents. The system sought to reduce the hardships of families whose main breadwinner was away from home – in some cases for many years – and also eased the worries of servicemen as it ensured their loved ones had a regular income. It also made service at sea more appealing, as there was nothing comparable in the Merchant Navy (with which the Royal Navy directly competed for labour) or the Army.

Men could either join the scheme by signing an allotment declaration at the time of volunteering or they could decide to opt into the scheme whenever the ship's company was mustered at sea.

Most of the records created by the scheme have long since been destroyed. However, some allotment registers and allotment declaration lists are at Kew. The allotment registers in ADM 27/1-21 (1795 to 1812) are large, heavy documents arranged by date and ship's name. As well as information about the man making the allotment, there are details of his family at home. In addition, his ship's book number – unique to each serviceman – is given. These are normally listed in a ship's muster or pay book, so they are an easy way to get into these records.

Allotment declaration lists in ADM 27/22-113 (1830 to 1851) are smaller, bound registers which include lists by ship's name and usually contain similar information as the allotment registers.

An index to ships in the registers is now available on TNA's online catalogue. You can also search by the rating's name, although at present only piece ADM 27/1, with 9,000 entries between 1795 and 1804, has been indexed by name.

There is more about these records in Bruno Pappalardo's article 'Caring from Afar', *Ancestors* (June 2009).

Trafalgar

If you think that the man you are researching was at the most famous British naval victory, the Battle of Trafalgar on 21 October 1805, then the Trafalgar Ancestors Database may well be of interest This little gem lists all those who fought in Nelson's fleet at the Battle of Trafalgar. This includes Royal Navy commissioned and warrant officers, ratings, supernumeraries and Royal Marines. Collectively, these individuals were born in a surprisingly wide range of continents and countries, for example, Africa, America, West Indies, India and most countries in Europe. Moreover, there is a reference to one Jane Townshend, the only woman positively identified as having served at Trafalgar.

In 1805, the Royal Navy employed around 110,000 individuals. So, if your ancestor served in the Royal Navy in 1805, there is roughly a one in six chance that they served at Trafalgar. The database can be searched by surname, but also using its advanced search facility, by first name, age on 21 October 1805, birthplace, ship's name, rating and rank.

The database is at www.nationalarchives.gov.uk/trafalgarancestors.

A related source is the Ayshford Trafalgar Roll (so called, because it is the result of the work of Pamela and Derek Ayshford), which contains the names of over 21,000 men who were listed on the musters of British ships at Trafalgar. The roll can be sampled on the Age of Nelson website (www.ageofnelson.org/TrafalgarRoll/index.html) and searched in full on CD. At the time of writing, the website suggests that the CD has sold out, but libraries, including the Society of Genealogists, may have copies.

The list is made up of both seamen and marines and usually provides a name, a ship and a rank. For some men, the age of the person and place of birth is available. In some cases, further material has been collected leading to more information on family, previous jobs, pensions, awards, medals, physical descriptions and pictures. One or two entries also contain details of injury, sickness and even time and place of death.

There are a few published biographical dictionaries telling the story of some of the men at Trafalgar, such as Tony Barrow's *Trafalgar Geordies and North Country Seamen of Nelson's Navy 1793–1815* (North East Press, 2005); there were well over fifty Geordies on the *Colossus* alone, for example.

Certificates of Service

Ratings (and warrant officers) who applied for a naval pension, a medal or gratuity had to provide a brief record of ships and dates, which were recorded in certificates of service compiled by the Navy Pay Office from the ships' pay books. They exist between 1802 and 1894. Many of the applications relate to orphaned children who wished to enter the Royal Greenwich Hospital School, so it can be assumed that in many cases the person for whom the application was being made was deceased. These certificates of service are found in books now in ADM 29/1-96.

The dates given in these books refer to the dates of issue of the certificates, which could be many years after a man had left the Navy. If the man was still serving, and later certificates were issued, this is noted in the entry books. You can currently search for a reference to an individual in ADM 29/1-73 using the catalogue. Type in the name of the person and restrict the search to ADM 29 in the 'Department or Series Code' box.

There were two sets:

- One which went to the Admiralty for the granting of pensions, superannuation, gratuities or medals.
- One sent to Royal Greenwich Hospital for the admission of children into the Lower School, otherwise known as the Royal Naval Asylum. These volumes relate to the fathers of children applying for entry to the school. The original certificates will be found among the Royal Greenwich Hospital School Admission Papers in ADM 73. (See also Chapter 2, and under Pensions below.)

Men Entering Between 1853 and 1872

The old system of recruiting men for particular voyages had many faults. In particular, it was always difficult to find enough men of sufficient calibre (hence the press gang). As new and more complicated technologies, such as the steam engine, were being introduced into the Navy it became clear it was necessary to recruit and retain a cadre of trained men to operate the new ships. In 1853, a new system was introduced by which men were recruited for a specific period, initially for ten years with the chance to extend by another ten years if the rating wished (and most did). Ratings already in the service could switch to the new system if they chose to.

From 1853 seamen entering the Navy were given a continuous service (CS) number. These were entered in Continuous Service Engagement Books (ADM 139 and online at DocumentsOnline). The books contain details of the individual's date and place of birth, physical characteristics on entry and a summary of service.

Some men served after 1873 and will have further entries in the Registers of Seamen's Service in ADM 188 (see below). There will be some certificates of service for these men in ADM 29 if they applied for pensions.

Men Entering between 1873 and 1923

Records of men who enlisted between 1873 and about 1923 (although a few records go up to the late 1920s) are in the Registers of Seamen's Services in ADM 188, and online through DocumentsOnline. For each man they give the date of birth, ship or shore establishment and a concise account of service, including successive appointments. You may find an entry on several pages, particularly for men who served for a long period

This seaman with a most impressive waxed moustache is a gunnery petty officer named Walter Ashcroft. On his right sleeve the man wears crossed guns with a star and king's crown above, showing he was either a gunnery instructor or gunner's mate. The medals, although worn on the left breast, do not appear to be official issues, nor are they medals awarded by the Royal Naval Temperance Society. They may be Masonic jewels. (Richard Taylor)

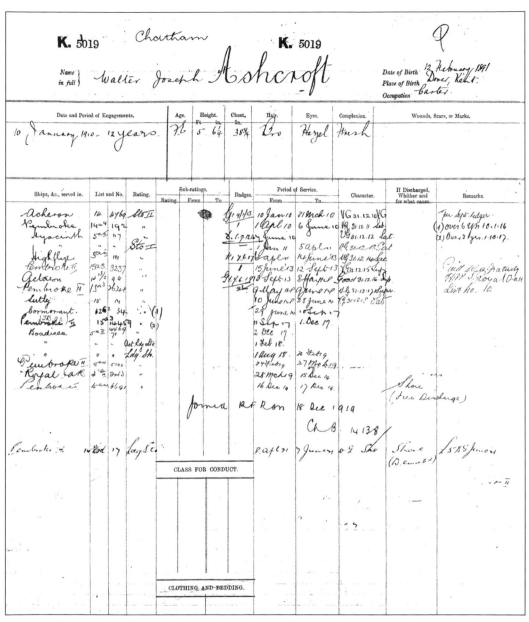

Walter Ashcroft's entry in the register of seaman's service. He was born at Dover in 1891 and on his discharge in December 1914 joined the Royal Fusiliers. (TNA ADM 188/877)

of time, or continued on another page already containing another man's service record.

Occasionally you will find a note on the register entry with a cross-reference to the 'new register'. These are in ADM 188/83-90, which continue entries appearing in earlier registers. If the rating entered before

1873 he may also have a CS number, so it is worth checking the records in ADM 139 (see above).

For men who served before 1894, it may also be worth checking the certificates of service in ADM 29 if they applied for pensions, etc. You can find out a little more about these records at www.portsmouth-genealogy. com/page14.htm.

Service Numbers

In 1894 and 1908 the Royal Navy made two major changes to the way service numbers were allocated. Before 1894, as a man joined the service into whatever branch, so he was allocated a number in sequence. In January 1894 it was decided that batches of numbers, representing particular branches, should be used so that anyone looking at a particular number would be able to know from which branch of the service the individual came from. The following sequences were used:

178001–240500	Seamen and Communications ratings
268001–273000	Engine Room Artificers
276001–313000	Stoker ratings
340001–348000	Artisans and Miscellaneous
350001–352000	Sick Berth Staff and Ship's Police
353001–366450	Officer's Stewards, Officer's Cooks and Boy Servants

In January 1908, the Royal Navy changed the service-number system again. Instead of having just numerical batches of service numbers for a given branch of the service, this time a new number sequence for each trade was started, with each branch assigned an alphabetical prefix:

F1	Royal Naval Air Service (July 1914–March 1918)
J 1–J 110000	Seamen and Communication ratings
M 1–M 38000	Engine Room Artificers
K 1–K 63500	Stokers
M 1–M 38000	Artisans and Miscellaneous
M 1–M 38000	Sick Berth Staff and Ship's Police
L 1–L 15000	Officer's Stewards, Officer's Cooks and Boy Stewards
SS 1–10000	Seamen (short service)
SS 100001–	Stokers (short service)
Y	Royal Naval Volunteer Reserve (1914–19)

In 1903 a new short-service system came into being, whereby individuals could join the RN for either 5 or 7 years, with the difference up to 12 (7 or 5 years) serving in the Royal Fleet Reserve. Service numbers starting with SS 1, served as Seamen, while service numbers beginning with SS 100001 were Stokers.

Service numbers commencing with a Y were given to men who enrolled in the Royal Naval Volunteer Reserve. If your man has only a Y number this indicates that he volunteered for service but was not actually called up, and his service record will not be found in ADM 188. However, it is possible to find entries with both a Y number and another service number. Where this occurs the man was called up for service, and the service record should be traceable in ADM 188 using the service number without the Y prefix.

Other Sources

Numerous records for ratings who roughly entered from the 1890s to the First World War are with the Fleet Air Arm Museum in Somerset; details are given in Appendix 2.

After 1923

Records of seamen who entered the Navy after 1923 are not held by TNA. To access these, you will need to contact RN Disclosure Cell, Room 48, West Battery, Whale Island, Portsmouth PO2 8DX. However, it is important to read the relevant pages on the Service Personnel and Veterans Agency website before you do (www.veterans-uk.info/service_records/service_records.html).

Pensions

Royal Greenwich Hospital

The Royal Hospital Greenwich was the naval equivalent of the Royal Hospital for old soldiers at Chelsea, and admitted its first forty-two residents in 1705. Numbers grew steadily, rising to 2,710 in 1814. Although they slept on beds instead of hammocks, their diet (based on bread, beer and boiled meat) would have reminded them of their days at sea. They took meals in the undercrofts below the Painted Hall and Chapel and were allowed to smoke their clay pipes, or 'chalks', in the Chalk Walk, now the Skittle Alley. The pensioners were given pocket

A view of one of the wards in the Royal Greenwich Hospital. (Simon Fowler)

money of 1s a week, which many of them supplemented by acting as guides for the many visitors to Greenwich and even as caddies at Blackheath Golf Club. You can find out more about the Hospital at http://tinyurl.com/28gchh3.

The Hospital also paid small out-pensions to large numbers of deserving applicants who had served in either the Navy or Royal Marines. Out-pensions were a form of superannuation in that claimants had to show former service in the Navy or Royal Marines, but there was no bar to them holding other employment, as the pensions were scarcely sufficient to live on. In 1763 it was fixed at £7 per annum. Many out-pensioners of the Hospital were still young men who found other employment. It was possible for both in and out-pensioners to re-enter the Navy, at which point their pensions lapsed until their discharge. There were some 30,000 such men on the books by 1820, costing more than £300,000 a year. In 1829 the costs were taken over entirely by the government.

The Hospital itself closed in the 1869 and the last inmates were sent to local hospitals. However, the charity behind it still exists with a website www.grenhosp.org.uk, which explains its current activities. The buildings themselves became the Royal Naval College for officers and are now the home of the University of Greenwich. There is a fascinating display on the history of the Hospital, including a mock-up of one of the 'cabins' in which the in-pensioners lived, in the Discover Greenwich Visitor Centre at the Old Royal Naval College.

Applications for entry into Royal Greenwich Hospital as an in-pensioner (that is as a resident) can be found in ADM 73. These records cover the period between 1790 and 1865 and are arranged by initial letter of surname. Some of these are indexed in more detail in TNA catalogue. Applications can contain service records and admission papers.

Applications for out-pensions (1737–1859) can be found in ADM 6/223-322. Records of payment of in-pensions are in ADM 73/36-41, 51-62 and applications and related paperwork to become in-pensioners in ADM 6/223-266, 267-268; ADM 65/83-97; ADM 73/1-35, 42-50, 63-69, 95-131. Payments of out-pensions are recorded in ADM 6/321; ADM 22/254-443; ADM 23/170; ADM 73/63-64, 95-131; PMG 71/5-13; PMG 72/1-2. For more details see Pappalardo or the In-depth Research Guide.

There are also a variety of miscellaneous records in ADM 80 which occasionally may be of interest.

Certificates of Service

To qualify for pensions, ratings had to prove their qualifying service, which they did by certificates issued by the Navy Pay Office. The certificate was an abstract of successive postings derived from the ships' musters. Before the introduction of continuous service registers for ratings, in the mid-nineteenth century, these certificates formed the only official evidence of the careers of ratings. Collections survive of both the original certificates as received by Greenwich, and of the Pay Office's entry books of the certificates as issued. The certificates of service give only the rating, the ships served in and the length of time in each. Those issued by the Navy Pay Office (1802–1919) are in ADM 29 and those by Royal Greenwich Hospital (1790–1865) are in ADM 73/1-35.

Service Pensions

In 1853 continuous service for ratings was introduced with the aim of granting a pension to all who served twenty years. The majority of ratings entered as boys, signing their first engagement at 18 and therefore retired at 38, or 43 for those who signed on for a 'fifth five'. This left a man with much of his working life remaining and naval pensioners were often still employed. The Navy employed pensioners in many duties as coastguards, in dockyards and other naval establishments (see Chapters 6 and 10). Few records of pensions to ratings survive but from the continuous service engagements and service registers it is possible to tell who received pensions (see above). But, surprisingly, often they joined the police, became prison warders or worked for the Poor Law authorities, where their experience of naval discipline and, for petty officers, man management undoubtedly proved invaluable.

Although unusual, it was not unknown for sailors to be unable to settle down after their discharge. If you can't find a death for your man or he appears to disappear for a number of years, it may be worth searching Poor Law and workhouse records, particular records of casual wards where tramps slept. Poor Law records are generally held locally, although some have been lost and there is no nationwide index. Ancestry is putting records for London online and Findmypast are beginning to do the same for Manchester, West Yorkshire and other areas. An introduction to the subject is at www.workhouses.org.uk or in Simon Fowler's An Introduction to Poor Law Records (Family History Partnership, 2011).

Wounds and Disability

Pensions for permanent disablement or grants to wounded ratings were paid by the Chatham Chest, on production of a certificate known as a smart ticket. For the period 1653–1799 records are in ADM 82; and for 1831–7, see ADM 22/52.

Widows' Pensions

The pay books of the Chatham Chest record payments of pensions to widows of ratings who died in service, between 1695 and 1779, are in ADM 82/12-119. A lump sum of one year's wages known as the Royal Bounty was payable to widows, dependant children or mothers (aged over 50) of ratings killed in action between 1675 and 1822. Papers submitted to claim the bounty often include marriage and death certificates, with other documents attesting the age, relationship or poverty of the applicants. Records are in ADM 106 and there is an index in the Open Reading Room. In addition, there are pay lists of the Royal Bounty between 1739 and 1787, giving name, address and relation of the payee, the name, quality and ship of the dead man, and the sum paid, and these are found in ADM 106/3018-3020, with later records between 1822 and 1917 in ADM 166.

If you are searching for the family of a seaman who became destitute as the result of his death then it might be worth trying the Library of the Naval History Museum in Portsmouth, which has the surviving papers of the Royal Navy Benevolent Society from 1791 until the 1968.

Memorials

It is far more difficult to find memorials to petty officers and other ranks than for officers. The best place to start out is the UK National Inventory of War Memorials, the database of which lists 60,000 war memorials. The vast majority of these are, of course, for the two world wars, but their database includes a number of memorials to naval personnel.

If your ancestor died in Malta then it is worth looking at the Malta Family History pages at http://tinyurl.com/63u97zn, which include brief details of some of the men who were buried on the island during the nineteenth and twentieth centuries. There are other interesting pages, including a list of Maltese men who served in the Royal Navy.

Courts Martial

Discipline was and is all-important on board ship, where crews might expect to live in close proximity to each other for months or even years, and where they were expected to do the captain's, and other officers', bidding unthinkingly, for otherwise *in extremis* the fate of the ship might depend on this loyalty. Unfortunately, certainly until the mid-nineteenth century, discipline was harsh, even by the standards of the day. It was based on the Articles of War, which were introduced in 1652. See the acknowledgements at the beginning of the book for an example of how thieves were punished.

Matters gradually changed during the nineteenth century, partly as a result of the abolition of the press gang, which meant that ratings generally wanted to be in the Navy. Even flogging, which was once the mainstay of naval discipline, was abolished in 1871. Even so, discipline remained harsh, although there was little evidence of rebelliousness by the lower decks. Things improved in the years before the First World War as the result of public pressure, with the major disciplinary offence, that of striking an officer (which theoretically was punished by death), being investigated more sympathetically and a reduction in the sentences meted out. As a result, the numbers of courts martial fell by two-thirds between 1900 and 1910.

Even so, officers could still mete out summary punishments without the need for any formal trial. Men could be summarily dismissed from the service, reduced to the ranks (known as 'derated'), given solitary confinement for up to a fortnight, deprived of the rum ration or even made to stand in a corner like a naughty schoolboy. Some naval officers were obsessed with cleanliness and many in the lower decks were punished for the odd speck of dust or for minor infringements with regard to the wearing of uniforms.

Officers were meant to be regulated by the *King's Regulations and Admiralty Instructions*, the voluminous pages of which contained guidance on almost every eventuality. But, in practice, a tyrannical commanding officer, or one who stuck rigorously to the rules, could get away almost with murder. As a result, discipline varied greatly from ship to ship. Petty officers and men were in constant fear of being derated or enduring pointless punishments without really knowing why. The situation began to change before the First World War when Winston Churchill, then First Lord of the Admiralty, pushed through changes that abolished the worst excesses and ensured that petty officers could only be derated after a court martial.

In addition, there was little understanding of the skills of man management, although the better captains and officers (notably Horatio Nelson) endeavoured to treat their crews decently and so were rewarded almost with adulation by their crews. Unfortunately, however, there were too many unthinking, unimaginative martinets, and this coupled with a large proportion of the crew who had been pressed and did not want to be on board was a recipe for trouble. Captain Bligh and HMS Bounty was the most extreme example, but in *Passage to Juneau* (Pantheon, 1999) the travel writer Jonathan Raban well-describes the simmering tensions between the officers that blighted George Vancouver's exploration of the Pacific Northwest in the 1790s in HMS *Discovery*.

Breaches of discipline were heard by courts martial formally constituted by the Admiralty. It was said that they only punished and they did not try, because they only concentrated on the immediate facts rather than considering any extenuating circumstances. It was only in the first decade of the twentieth century that the defendant was allowed to give evidence in his own defence or allow a 'prisoner's friend' to represent him.

Records of courts marital are largely in ADM 1. For between 1680 and 1839 they are in pieces 5353-5494. From 1845 to 1910 they are arranged by year. No records between 1840 and 1844 are known to survive. Some earlier records are in pieces HCA 55/1-3 (for officers between 1802 and 1856), ADM 106/3074 and ADM 13/103-104.

Details of courts martial from between about 1680 and 1702 for both officers and ratings are now available through the online catalogue and reflect the draconian discipline found on board at the period. For example, Herbert Boyle, a seaman on HMS Tiger, was court-martialled in June 1684 and found guilty of 'deserting his station and neglect of duty'. He was sentenced to be 'flogged around the fleet and receive nine lashes on his bare back with a cat of nine tails at each of HMS *Mordant*; HMS *Sandades*; HMS *Phoenix*; HMS *Centurion*; HMS *Deptford*; HMS *Charlotte* and 31 lashes at HMS *Tiger*' (ADM 1/5283, ff. 27–8). Occasionally, the offences appear to be trivial, but perhaps reflect the fact of an unhappy ship where discipline and respect have all but broken down, as may have been the case with Thomas Pope, a gunner in HMS Chester, who was tried in March 1701 for 'keeping his wife and child on board for 18 months, taking beer ashore, using indecent expressions about the commander'. He was found guilty only of using indecent expressions about the commander and fined two weeks' pay (ADM 1/5261, f. 213).

There are also registers of courts martial in ADM 194 and these run from 1812 to 1978 with separate registers for officers and for petty officers and ratings. Don't forget that courts may have sat some time after the offence was committed. There are, in fact, several series of records for courts martial that took place in the twentieth century. Those for courts martial from 1890 are in ADM 156: files in this series are closed for seventy-five years from the date of the court martial, that is records of trials from 1935 were opened in 2011, 1936 in 2012 and so forth, although it is not clear from the catalogue what is available and what is not. Also of interest are courts martial records in ADM 178, which run between 1892 and 1951. Again, the more recent material is likely to be closed for seventy-five years. The system and the records are explained in more detail in Pappalardo.

Women at Sea

Until well into the Napoleonic Wars ships often carried small numbers of wives (actual or 'nominal') of crew members who were often employed to do the washing and carry out elementary nursing in battle. Their presence on board depended on the captain's good will. Very little is known about these women because they are almost never listed in official records, although just possibly it may be worth looking through any list of supernumeraries in the muster books at TNA (ADM 36–ADM 38). Just one woman – Jane Townshend – appears in TNA's Trafalgar Ancestors Database. In her application for a Naval General Service Medal in 1847 (which was rejected) she claims to have performed 'useful services' on HMS *Defiance* during the engagement, which would have involved nursing the wounded. Other women, such as Ann Hopping and Mary Ann Riley, also claimed the Medal for having been present at the Battle of the Nile in 1798, which the Admiralty declined fearing 'innumerable applications' from others. But the practice of allowing women on board during voyages came to the end as the result of increasing concerns about morals on board from evangelical campaigners (who included a number of naval officers) and changing attitudes to women in society as a whole.

Women, in the form of the WRNS, were not officially employed on board naval vessels until the Second World War, and then only in very limited roles (see Chapter 5). And full shipboard equality was not granted until 1993. However, before then very, very occasionally women enlisted as sailors, making sure to keep their gender secret. Of course, we know next to nothing about them, although there are several interesting articles on the subject by the Historical Maritime Society at www.hms.org.uk and the BBC at http://tinyurl.com/6yosn3b.

One exception was Mary Lacey (or Lacy) who wrote her autobiography, giving us a detailed picture of life as a sailor aboard a warship. In 1759 she went to sea in men's clothes as William Chandler, an apprentice carpenter, on board HMS *Sandwich*, but was hospitalised with rheumatism. In 1763 Miss Lacey decided to become a shipwright's apprentice based at Portsmouth dockyard and gained her certificate in 1770 despite being discovered and confessing she was a woman to two male colleagues, who surprisingly swore to keep her secret. However, rheumatoid arthritis meant she was no longer able to work in such a physically demanding environment and in order to obtain a pension she revealed her identity as Mary Lacey. Perhaps surprisingly, her petition was successful and she retired with a pension of £20 per annum, publishing her story as *The History of the Female Shipwright* (which has recently been republished by the National Maritime Museum). You can find more at http://tinyurl.com/6hpo74d, where there is a link to a podcast about her career. Mary Lacey also warrants a short if rather unsympathetic entry in the *Oxford Dictionary of National Biography*.

Chapter 5

THE NAVY AFTER 1914

The twentieth century saw the Navy expand to its greatest extent and also contract to a size probably not seen since Elizabethan days. It took on new challenges and technologies, such as submarines, flight and, in the post-war years, nuclear missiles. But even today the traditions remain strong and the organisation and way of doing things has adapted with surprising ease to whatever challenges have presented themselves.

Many of the records described below cover both world wars, so if you are just researching ancestors who served in the Second World War it is also worth reading the section for the First World War as well. Sea Your History is an excellent website about the history of the Royal Navy in the twentieth century (although there is a little earlier material) maintained

The Second Battle Squadron prepare for action before the Battle of Jutland, May 1916. (National Museum of the Royal Navy)

by the Royal Naval Museum at www.seayourhistory.org.uk, with sections on the dockyards, discipline and life on board.

First World War

In 1914 Britain had the largest and most powerful navy in the world. Yet it is a paradox that at the only major naval battle of the war (at Jutland in May 1916) it failed to prove its dominance in an indecisive encounter with the German Grand Fleet. For many men the greatest enemy was boredom.

The Navy's fighting qualities were not exemplified in fleet actions (of which there were very few) as much as in single-ship operations where skill and daring were given free rein. The exploits of British submariners were legendary. Max Horton, commanding submarine E9, terrorised German shipping in the Baltic to such an extent that the area became known as 'Horton's Sea' and the Germans resorted to recruiting a female assassin, who unfortunately succumbed to his charms.

Q-ships, which posed as unarmed merchantmen, were another way in which men could show their abilities under fire. 'Panic parties', for example, were trained to simulate 'panic' to give the impression that the ship was being abandoned. If a U-boat came close enough to the supposed 'abandoned' ship then it would be engaged by the concealed gun crews still on board.

For the most part during the latter stages of the war naval ships were engaged in the dull but vital task of protecting convoys bringing essential food and supplies from North America and further afield. Convoys were only introduced in 1917 after considerable opposition from the Admiralty. The new system dramatically cut the loss of merchant shipping from enemy attack and almost certainly saved Britain from a humiliating collapse in early 1918.

There are two excellent websites that offer histories of the Royal Navy during the war: www.worldwar1.co.uk and www.worldwar1atsea.net.

Service Records

Brief details of officers can be found in the published *Navy Lists*. A set can be found on the shelves in the Open Reading Room at Kew. TNA also has a set of the *Confidential Navy Lists*, which contain more information, such as where an officer was serving, in series ADM 177.

The Continuous Service Record of Petty Officer Ernest Highams. He was killed in the first weeks of the war in an action with the German light cruiser Königsberg off East Africa in HMS Pegasus. (TNA ADM 136/240)

56

162971   D'port.

Name in full	Ernest Edward **Highams**
Date of Birth	7 May 1876
Place of Birth	Charlton, Dover
Occupation	Butcher

Date and Period of C. S. Engagements.	Age.	Height. Ft. in.	Hair.	Eyes.	Complexion.	Wounds, Scars, Marks, &c.
7 May 1894 — 12 years						
7 May 1906 — To comp. vol						

Ships, &c., served in.	List and No.	Rating.	Sub-ratings. Rating.	Sub-ratings. From	To	Badges.	Period of Service. From	Period of Service. To	Character.	If Discharged, Whither and for what Cause.
Impregnable	13c II 19	P.O. 2cl	G.II	trans		2B (Keng)			VG 21·12·10 VG	
Gibraltar	5² 24	"	G.P II	trans	G1 26·10·09	14 May 10			VG 31·12·11 Supr.	
Pyramus	5¹ 9	P.O.1s	P.9	trans	31·10·10	3.	1 Nov 10		VG trans Pyt.	
Pegasus	··	"		(1)			16 Feb 11	9 Nov 11	VG 31·12·13 Pyt.	
							10 Nov 11	20 Sep 14	VG Ex Dt. as below	

N. P. 2161/14.
D.D. 20 Sep 1914.
Killed in action with German
cruiser "Königsberg".

TRACED WAR GRATUITY BY No.

Class for Conduct.

Clothing and Bedding Gratuities.		REMARKS.

10/11·93 Passed professionally for P.O (2s) 7/4/09

✓ Per. Pegasus mchv.
(1) Over Pys 31·10·13

PAID WAR GRATUITY

Service records for officers and the non-commissioned warrant officers who served during the war are at Kew in pieces ADM 196/97-114, with a partial index in ADM 313/110. Here you should find details of an officer's family and his date of birth, promotions and ships served on, together with brief notes about a man's performance. Another useful series are the summaries of confidential reports also in ADM 196, which contain candid comments on officers' abilities written by senior officers. These records are on DocumentsOnline.

Also worth checking out is ADM 340 which contains files and record-of-service cards, describing the service of officers in the Royal Navy, the Royal Naval Reserve, the Royal Naval Volunteer Reserve and the Women's Royal Naval Service (WRNS), arranged in alphabetical order. Cards and files were introduced early in the twentieth century for all officers then serving. These documents form a single continuous record spanning the length of the officer's service. A few records in this series include service through the two world wars and into the 1950s. An index to officers who appear in here can be found in TNA's online catalogue, although at the time of writing it is not complete.

Claims for pensions for wounds are in PMG 23/206-207 and PMG 42/13-14.

Records of ratings are in ADM 188 and online through Documents Online. These rather disappointing records will tell you which ships a man served with, medals won and perhaps what happened to him, promotions and remarks about conduct. Records for ratings who served with a section of armoured cars in Russia between 1915 and 1917 are in ADM 116/529.

There are several series of records that include material about pensions awarded to naval personnel who served in the war. A small number of widows' pension applications are in PIN 82. PMG 56/1-9 has details of allowances made to widows, dependants and children of specially entered mercantile crews, and crews of mercantile ships commissioned as HM ships or auxiliary craft, who were killed during naval warlike operations. And details of pensions awarded to officers and men of the mercantile marine killed or injured in Admiralty employment are in PIN 15/1733-1736, while claims to pension from members of the Royal Naval Reserve are in PIN 15/209-211.

The Fleet Air Arm Museum (see Appendix 2) has engagement books for men who joined between 1905 and 1921. These books include details of date and place of joining, physical description, details of any previous military service and parent's consent if the entrant was a boy.

Casualties

Although we might think that the Commonwealth War Graves Commission (CWGC) is only responsible for the immaculate and moving war graves of the First World War in Northern France and Flanders, in fact it is responsible for war graves of Commonwealth personnel from each of the services from 1914 to the present. Naval officers and ratings with no known graves – about two-thirds of the total – are commemorated on huge naval memorials at Chatham, Portsmouth and Plymouth. But wherever they lie today the men are recorded on the Debt of Honour Register, which is online at www.cwgc.org.

The Register is an invaluable source for both world wars. Entries for individuals will usually give the rank and service number, the ship or unit and the date of death. Particularly for the Second World War, you may also find the names of their parents and a home address. Incidentally, the Register also has details of civilians who lost their lives during Second World War bombing raids including the victims of raids on Portsmouth, Plymouth and other naval ports. The website also provides information about the cemeteries where the men are buried or commemorated and gives the exact location of their grave or name on a memorial to the missing.

CWGC
Commonwealth War Graves Commission

Casualty Details

Name:	HIGHAMS
Initials:	E E
Nationality:	United Kingdom
Rank:	Petty Officer
Regiment/Service:	Royal Navy
Unit Text:	H.M.S. "Pegasus."
Date of Death:	20/09/1914
Service No:	162971
Casualty Type:	Commonwealth War Dead
Cemetery:	ZANZIBAR (GRAVE ISLAND) CEMETERY

Search Page | Certificate

Home | Site Map | Contact Us | Useful Links | Debt of Honour | Privacy Policy | Terms and Conditions | Credits

Home

The entry for Ernest Highams in the Commonwealth War Graves Commission Debt of Honour Register. (Commonwealth War Graves Commission)

Grave Island, off Zanzibar, where Petty Officer Highams is buried. The cemetery is one of the least accessible maintained by the Commonwealth War Graves Commission, which advises visitors that 'there are no landing stages and visitors will normally have to wade out to, and in from, the boat. Visitors at low tide will also have to walk 50 metres or more across mud and very slippery rocks. Appropriate dress and beach shoes should be worn.' (Commonwealth War Graves Commission)

There are several projects that photograph war graves, including those of naval personnel. One of the largest is the War Graves Photographic Project (http://twgpp.org).

Details of some 45,000 Royal Navy and Royal Marine officers and ratings who died during the First World War are listed in the War Graves Roll in ADM 242. The Roll gives full name, rank, service number, ship's name, date and place of birth, cause of death, where buried and next of kin. The records are now available online through Findmypast. The Roll was based on a card index which is also in ADM 242, which also gives the place of burial, such as 'Buried [in] East Africa on a small knoll marked by blazed tree, R. bank Kaibiga River, 100 yards W. of Ndyimbwa-Ungwara'. For those who fell serving at Gallipoli there are often detailed descriptions rather than traditional locations for the grave. Further registers of killed and wounded are in ADM 104/145-149.

180
Roll :-

Name	Rank or Rating	No.	Medals, &c., earned				How Issued or disposed of	Remarks
HIGHAM, Wm.	P.O.	196248		Sr	V	B	H.M. CGd, Queenstown	
" Wm.	L.S.	J.36450		Sr	V	B	"Victory"	
" Wm.	L.Sto.	K.19743		Sr	V	B	S	
" Wm.	Sto.1.	S.S.105016	Rjns Scc		V	B	S	
" Wm. E.	A.M.2.	F.50167				B	By A.M.	
HIGHAMS, Edgar J.	M.A.A.	180760		Sr	V	B	S	
" Ernest E.	P.O.	162971		Sr	V	B	FR	LC 1011/1911
" Wm. R.	O.S.2.	L.7310			V	B	S	
HIGHBRE, Edgar W.	E.R.A.1.	269531		Sr	V	B	S	
HIGH-CASTON, Robt. H.	Boy.2.	J.35026				B		
HIGHCOCK, Robt.	A.B.	J.44808			V	B	S	
HIGHDALE, Wm. H.	A.B.	J.1040		Sr	V	B	"Lucia"	
HIGHET, Geo.	E.R.A.3.	M.21013			V	B	MR	LC 1151/1914
HIGHFIELD, Arthur G.	Jr.4.	M.22469				B	S	
" Chas.	A.B.	S.S.3681		Sr	V	B	S	
" Fredk.	Sto.2.	K.51209			V	B	S	
" Henry E.	Jr.4.	M.16465			V	B	S	
" John	O.E.R.A.1.	165413		Sr	V	B	S	
" John	L.Sto.	S.S.112250		Sr	V	B	S	
" John T.	A.C.1.	F.14485				B		
" Wm.	Shpt.2.	343930		Sr	V	B	"Pembroke"	
" Wm.	Sto.1.	S.S.110829		Sr	V	B	F	R
" Wm. C.	Act. A.M.1/	F.35315				B		
HIGHLAND, Stephen J.	Sto.1.	K.1384		Sr	V	B	F	R
" Wm. F.	A.B.	212618		Sr	V	B	S	

Ernest Highams' entry in the First World War campaign medal rolls. (Ancestry/TNA ADM 171/105)

In addition, naval casualties are listed in: S. D. and D. B. Jarvis, *The Cross of Sacrifice: Officers who Died in the Service of the RN, RNVR, RM, RNAS and RAF, 1914–1919* (Naval & Military Press, 2000) and S. D. and D. B. Jarvis, *The Cross of Sacrifice: Non-Commissioned Officers, Men and Women of the UK, Commonwealth and Empire Who Died in the Service of the Royal Naval Air Service, Royal Navy, Royal Marines, Royal Flying Corps and*

Royal Air Force, 1914–1921 (Naval & Military Press, 1996). TNA and Society of Genealogists libraries have copies of these books. Lists of casualties can also be found on the Naval History Net website: http://www.naval-history.net/xDKCas1003-Intro.htm. These cover the whole of the twentieth century.

A roll of honour recording the 7,000 officers and men who died at Jutland with some details of their career is published by Family History Indexes. Details are at www.fhindexes.co.uk/jutland.htm. There were many rolls of honour published in the years after the First World War which recorded the sacrifice made by sailors as well as soldiers. There is no national collection, but both the Imperial War Museum and Society of Genealogists have reasonable accumulations and a number are online at www.roll-of-honour.com.

There are some 60,000 war memorials across the United Kingdom, the vast majority of which are for the two world wars (especially of course for the First World War), and your sailor ancestor may appear on one or more. The UK National Inventory of War Memorials (www.ukniwm. org.uk) describes them all, including 550 specifically dedicated to men of the Royal Navy. Unfortunately, there is no national index to names, but there are a surprising number of people researching the men who appear on local memorials. Some of these individuals have set up useful websites. Otherwise the local studies library or archive should be able to put you in contact with local researchers.

Prisoners of War

Unfortunately, it is difficult to find out very much about individual POWs, largely because detailed Red Cross registers and other records were lost in the late 1920s. A list of prisoners in German and Turkish hands in 1916 is in AIR 1/892/204/5/696-698, which indicates where the prisoner was captured and when, where they were held and their next of kin. There is a published *List of Officers taken Prisoner in the Various Theatres of War between August 1914 and November 1918* (1919, repr. London Stamp Exchange, 1988) which includes a number of naval officers. Copies are in TNA and Society of Genealogists libraries. A selection of interrogation reports of prisoners of war when they were repatriated to Britain in 1918 are in WO 161 and online through DocumentsOnline. There is also some correspondence in ADM 1, ADM 116, ADM 137 and FO 383, with an index to correspondence in ADM 12 (code 79).

Medals and Awards

Naval personnel were entitled to the same campaign medals as their military counterparts. Rolls for these medals are in ADM 171 and online through Ancestry, although they contain much less detail than the Army's Medal Information Cards. ADM 171 also contains details of medals awarded for gallantry. Biographies of naval VC winners and the reasons behind the award of the medal can be found in Stephen Snelling's *The Naval VCs of the First World War* (Sutton Publishing, 2002).

Operational Records

It can be frustratingly difficult to track down reports and descriptions of activities during the First World War. If you can get hold of a copy, perhaps the best place to start is with the Official Histories. TNA has a complete set and other large libraries should have copies. In addition, Naval & Military Press has reprinted many volumes.

Ships' log books (in ADM 53, with submarines in ADM 173) normally only include weather and navigational details. Perhaps of more immediate use are the brief histories of most Royal Navy ships, which are at www.battleships-cruisers.co.uk/royal.htm. It is also worth checking to see whether there is an entry in Wikipedia. A project to put some of these logs online is at www.oldweather.org.

Otherwise, material might be found in three other series, although TNA's online catalogue might be able to assist you in your search. ADM 137 contains most of the Admiralty papers for the period and is the best place to start. If this is unsuccessful try ADM 116 and then ADM 1.

The Inter-war Period and Second World War

Service Records

Service records for both officers and ratings who served in the Royal Navy after 1924 are still held by the Ministry of Defence. Veterans and next of kin can request copies for which a charge, currently £30, is made (although this may be waived for veterans themselves and their widows). More details are given on the helpful and informative website of the Service Personnel and Veterans Agency at www.veterans-uk.info.

All Royal Navy personnel were given their service record when they were discharged. For pension purposes the Navy retained pay details. Therefore, the only information held for seamen and officers are their

The White Ensign flies proudly over an unidentified warship of the Second World War.
(Crown Copyright)

service details (number, rank, name, etc.) and a list of dates when they served on ships and or shore bases. For details contact: DPS(N)2, Building 1/152, PP65 Victory View, HMNB Portsmouth PO1 3LS.

Each rating's service number had a combination of letters before it signifying the branch he was with and designated port. The abbreviations for branches were:

J (Seamen), K (Stokers), L (Stewards and Cooks), M (Miscellaneous), and for ports: C (Chatham), D (Devonport), F (Fleet Air Arm) and P (Portsmouth). In addition, the letter X meant that the individual adhered to the new pay code introduced in 1925, and the S meant special service engagement (that is for the duration of the war).

Officers

As well as the published *Navy Lists* there is a series of *Confidential Navy Lists*, which indicate where individual officers were serving, with the names of ships and establishments. These can be found in ADM 177.

Some summaries of confidential reports on captains and their suitability for promotion up until 1943 are in pieces ADM 196/93-94. Photographs are attached to reports. Records for honorary officers who served in the RNR are in ADM 240. Biographies of a number of Second World War naval officers can be found at www.unithistories.com/officers/RN_officersW2.html.

Medals

Recommendations for gallantry medals to members of the Royal Navy and Royal Marines are in ADM 1/29358-30077, 30098-30984 (with an index in ADM 12) and ADM 116. Lists of naval recipients of the Victorian and George crosses are in ADM 1/23187 and George Medal (GM) in ADM 171/164-165. A register listing VC winners from all services is available on DocumentsOnline; access is free.

Lists of men who were awarded gallantry medals, together with service number and date the event was gazetted, can be found in the appropriate volume of *Seedie's Roll of Naval Honours and Awards 1939–1959* (Ripley Registers, 1989), *Seedie's list of Coastal Forces Awards for World War II* (Ripley Registers, 1992) and *Seedie's List of Submarine Awards for World War II* (Ripley Registers, 1990). TNA Library has the volume for submarines.

Officers and ratings were entitled to one or more campaign medals depending on which theatres of war they saw action in. There were eight separate campaign medals issued, although no more than five could be worn by an individual. As a cost-saving measure, medals were not inscribed with the names of the individuals to whom they were awarded, although a number of individuals subsequently had inscriptions added privately. The medals that could have been awarded to naval personnel were:

Medal	Notes
1939–45 Star	This was the basic war service star and was generally awarded to men who had completed six months' active service overseas. It was the only medal awarded to men who saw service in France and Norway in 1940 and Greece and Crete in 1941. Those awarded this star were eligible for others if they served in other theatres of operation.
Atlantic Star	Generally awarded to the RN and Merchant Navy who served in convoys across the North Atlantic, but members of the RAF and Army attached to the RN and Merchant Navy also received it.
Africa Star	Awarded for one or more day's service anywhere in North Africa before 12 May 1943.
Burma Star	Awarded for service in India and Burma.
Italy Star	Awarded for service in Italy, the Balkans and Southern France between 11 June 1943 and 8 May 1945.
Pacific Star	Awarded for operational service in the Pacific Theatre of Operations between 8 December 1941 and 2 September 1945. Also awarded to personnel who served in Hong Kong, Malaya and Sumatra.
Defence Medal	Awarded to all those who served in a military capacity in Britain, Malta and British colonies between September 1939 and May 1945, including civilians and members of the Home Guard.
War Service Medal	Issued to anyone who rendered twenty-eight days in uniform or in an accredited organisation.

Unless they were still serving when the medals were issued, former service personnel had to apply for them, although not everybody did. Veterans can still apply and next of kin can ask for replacement medals. You need to contact the MoD Medal Office, Building 250, Imjin Barracks, Gloucester GL3 1HW; tel: 014 1224 3600; http://tiny.cc/q2pzc. The informative website contains copies of the forms you will need to fill in. The medal rolls themselves are not yet at TNA. There's an interesting page explaining what medals were awarded during the war at www.petergh.f2s.com/medals.htm (the rest of the site is worth exploring too).

Details of ratings who were awarded the Conspicuous Gallantry Medal (CGM) are listed in P. McDermott's *For Conspicuous Gallantry – the Register of the Conspicuous Gallantry Medal, 1855–1958* (Naval & Military Press, 1998). Medal rolls for the Distinguished Service Cross (DSC) are in ADM 171/164-165, and a similar list for officers of the RNR is in BT 164/23.

Medal rolls for the Distinguished Service Medal (DSM) from 1942 only are in ADM 171/164-165. However, all recipients are listed in W. H. Fevyer's *The Distinguished Service Medal 1939–1946* (Hayward, 1981). Lists of men who were awarded the Long Service and Good Conduct Medal during the war are in ADM 171 and on Ancestry.

The service records for the Royal Naval Reserve contain papers on awards to RNR officers. These documents are in BT 164.

Casualty Records

As well as the resources of the Commonwealth War Graves Commission (see above), there are several sources specifically for the Royal Navy. The most important of which are two typescript lists held by the Department of Printed Books at the Imperial War Museum: 'Names of Officers who Died during the Period beginning 3rd September 1939 and ending 30th June 1948' and the 'Register of Deaths (Naval Ratings) 3rd September 1939 to 30th June 1948'. A set is also held by the Royal Naval Museum Library. Servicemen are listed by surname, together with official number, branch of service, ship and date and place of birth and death, and occasionally details of medals awarded or other information.

Reports of death other than that from enemy action of individuals are to be found in series ADM 104/105-107, 127-139 (ratings only) arranged by ship. Again, details of service number, ship and place and date of birth and death (and its cause) are given.

A list of RNR officers killed or wounded during the war is in BT 164/23. Details of RNR and RNVR medical officers who were killed between 1939 and 1946 are in ADM 261/1.

Lists of casualties can also be found on the Naval History Net website: http://www.naval-history.net/xDKCas1003-Intro.htm.

Sick and Wounded

Surgeons' journals, compiled by doctors on board ships and in some hospitals, can be found in ADM 101. These journals contain an account of the treatment of medical and surgical cases, and usually a copy of the daily sick list, statistical abstracts of the incidence of diseases and general comments on the health and activities of the ship's company. They are arranged by ship or shore station. However, for data protection reasons, the vast majority have not yet been released to the public. ADM 261/1 also includes reports of medical treatment to survivors of RN ships either sunk or badly damaged by enemy action.

Prisoners of War

Lists of Royal Navy personnel interned in enemy prisoner of war camps may be found in many of the files in ADM 1 (code 79) and ADM 116 (code 79), although the exact files are not identifiable from the catalogue.

A list of Fleet Air Arm prisoners of war in Germany and occupied Europe is at www.fleetairarmarchive.net/RollofHonour/POW/Camp_ list.htm.

Operational Records

Operational records can be found in three series:

- ADM 199 – case papers relating to all sorts of naval activities from convoys to captain's reports on damage done to individual ships.
- ADM 1 – Admiralty and Secretariat Papers, arranged by subject (called codes).
- ADM 116 – more secret and important papers gathered by the Admiralty and bound together in cases. As with ADM 1, they are arranged by subject codes.

In practice, there seems to be no hard and fast rule about which records are to be found where, although it is best to start by going through ADM 199. Fortunately, TNA online catalogue makes the search much simpler than was once the case. It now includes detailed indexes to a number of records, including details of convoys and the ships that sailed in them.

Most RN effort during the war was directed towards protecting convoys crossing the North Atlantic. Although often tedious work, this was vital to the war effort. Records of convoys are in ADM 237 and to a lesser extent in other series such as ADM 199 and ADM 217. They are normally arranged by the code name assigned to individuals, such as

PQ17, where PQ signified convoys sailing between Iceland and Archangel in Russia and 17 the 17th convoy in the sequence. Lists of these prefixes can be found on Wikipedia, but a more comprehensive introduction is Arnold Hague's Convoy Database at www.convoyweb.org.

More information can be found in the TNA In-depth Research Guide *Royal Navy: Operational Records: Second World War, 1939–1945*. But probably of more immediate use are two excellent websites devoted to the Second World War. Despite its name, Uboat.net has many pages devoted to the role of the RN in the North Atlantic (www.uboat.net). Another invaluable source is the Naval History Net at (www.naval-history.net).

The Caird Library, at the National Maritime Museum, has a large collection relating to the retreat from Dunkirk in 1940. In particular, it has 'The Dunkirk List (Dunkirk Withdrawal: Operation Dynamo May 26–June 4,

Ratings relax in their mess on board a corvette. (*News Chronicle*)

1940: Alphabetical List of Vessels Taking Part, With Their Services', which was compiled by Lt Col G. P. Orde immediately after the evacuation was completed, using all available sources, official and private, and includes numerous interviews with survivors. Orde gives an account of every vessel taking part in Operation DYNAMO, arranged in alphabetical order by name. Some general subject headings are included in the sequence, such as 'blockships', 'flare burning drifters', 'minesweeper groups' and 'routes to Dunkirk', and cross-references are given where necessary.

Records of Ships (see also Chapter 7)

Surviving ships' logs are in ADM 53, although ones for ships smaller than cruisers do not appear to have survived, apart from for 1939 and the early months of 1940. It is easy to find out which logs have survived by typing the name of the vessel into TNA online catalogue.

Ship's movements can be traced via a series of lists:

- Pink Lists (ADM 187) – regularly printed lists, usually compiled every three or four days, showing where each ship was stationed or their movements, with dates of arrival and departure.
- Red Lists (ADM 208) – weekly lists of all minor vessels in home waters, arranged by command.
- Blue Lists (ADM 209) – ships under construction.
- Green Lists (ADM 210) – weekly lists of landing craft and similar vessels in home waters and foreign stations, arranged by command.

Sets may also be found in the Royal Naval Museum and National Maritime Museum libraries.

Captain's letters and reports of proceedings contain information relating to the activities of naval vessels, in the form of letters from the commanding officer (Captain's Letters) or Reports of Proceedings (R of P) submitted to the Admiralty. These are probably the most informative source if you are researching a particular incident. Unfortunately, they are not found together in a single source, but are scattered through ADM 1 and ADM 199. You may find them arranged by ship or by operation or convoy.

If you want to know more about the loss of a particular ship then you may need to use John M. Young's *Britain's Sea War: A Diary of Ship Losses, 1939–1945* (Patrick Stephens, 1989), which lists all ships, military and civilian, lost during the war. It is based on two official government publications: *Ships of the Royal Navy: Statement of Losses during the Second World War* (HMSO, 1947) and *British Merchant Vessels Lost or Damaged by Enemy Action during Second World War* (HMSO, 1947). Brief descriptions of each RN ship lost, and the reason for its loss, can also be found at www.naval-history.net.

A court martial was held after the loss of a ship and these records are for the most part in ADM 1, although they are closed for seventy-five years.

The Submarine Service

In general, records for submarines and submariners are very similar to those of the rest of the Navy. Submarine logs are in ADM 173, which record all wheel, telegraph and depth-keeping orders, and details of battery charges, torpedo firing and navigation. They were kept by crew members otherwise engaged in steering or depth keeping, and contain many abbreviated references. Some logs are humorously annotated with notes and drawings. War patrol reports and associated records, arranged by boat, are in ADM 236, with some records in ADM 199.

The Royal Navy Submarine Museum has substantial archives of papers, both official and private, relating to the service. Of particular interest is the material relating to individual vessels. Also of use are the Movement Record Cards for ratings for the two world wars and the interwar period which indicate which boats a man served on. Their website also has pages devoted to the loss of individual submarines at sea (see Appendix 5 for details).

John Atkinson's *Royal Navy Submarine Service Losses in WWII* (Galago, 2004) is a comprehensive record of the names of all the men who lost their lives during submarine service in the Second World War. The book includes details of each submarine lost (from HMS/m *Oxley* in 1939 to HMS/m *Porpoise* in 1945), the reason, date and the commanding officer, together with each member of the crew who died, his name, rank and any decorations awarded.

After 1945

The Royal Navy has continued to play a prominent role in the defence of Britain and within NATO. Although much shrunken in size, it remains the fourth biggest Navy in the world. Had the cold war turned warm, it would have been responsible for keeping the North Atlantic safe for convoys crossing the ocean. The Royal Navy also controls Britain's nuclear capacity in the form of Polaris and Trident missiles carried in nuclear submarines. In addition, the Navy has played a part in many other conflicts around the world from the Yangtze Incident of 1949, involving HMS *Amethyst*, to patrolling the coastal waterways of southern Iraq in the mid-2000s. However, the Falklands War of 1982 was undoubtedly the Navy's greatest moment since 1945.

Finding information about the activities of the Royal Navy in this period, and the men and women who sailed on its ships, can be frustrating. The thirty-year rule means that government records are normally closed after the early 1980s, although the government has recently decided to the close documents for twenty years in future, although it will be a few years before this is introduced. In addition, many operational records are closed for longer periods, usually fifty or seventy-five years. And, of course, personnel records are still with the MoD.

However, the best place to start researching what your mother or grandfather did in the post-war period is almost certainly the Internet. The excellent Britain's Small Wars website (http://www.britains-smallwars.com), for example, has much about the various conflicts all the services found themselves in, as well as some useful links to other sites. In addition, the Naval History Net (http://www.naval-history.net/) also has some material. There are also a plethora of websites devoted to individual ships and the crews who served on them. Often they are more an exercise in nostalgia rather than anything analytical. A search on Google should come up with something. There are also websites through which you can contact former comrades, such as Servicepals (http://servicepals.co.uk) and Forces Reunited (www.forcesreunited.org.uk).

The new Armed Forces Memorial website has a roll of honour that allows you to search for naval personnel who have died since 1948. This can be found at www.veterans-uk.info/amf2/index.php.

Details of service personnel buried in 'non-world war' graves are available from the Joint Casualty and Compassionate Centre, Service Personnel and Veterans Agency, Imjin Barracks, Innsworth, Gloucester GL3 1HW. Please mark your enquiry 'Graves Casework'.

At TNA, ships' logs are available to the end of 1981 (series ADM 53). Admiralty correspondence continues to be added to ADM 1 and

ADM 116. Increasingly, the Royal Navy was working more and more closely with the other services at this point so it may be worth looking at the Chiefs of Staff papers in DEFE 4 and DEFE 5, although these records are more to do with policy than operational records.

Sources for the study of the post-war Navy held by TNA are described in an In-depth Research Guide, *Royal Navy: operations and policy after 1945*.

Royal Naval Air Services

Royal Naval Air Service (RNAS)

Naval aviation began in a very small way with the gift of two aircraft from the Royal Aero Club through one of its members, Francis McLean, in November 1910. The Club also offered to train pilots at its base at Eastchurch on the Isle of Sheppey. The Royal Flying Corps was established in April 1912 to develop both military and naval aviation in general. It was under the control of the Army. The Navy wing broke away a few weeks before the outbreak of the First World War and was named the Royal Naval Air Service. The new service had 93 aircraft, 6 airships, 2 balloons and 727 personnel.

During the First World War the main roles of the RNAS were fleet reconnaissance, patrolling coasts for enemy ships and submarines, attacking enemy coastal territory and defending Britain from enemy air raids, along with deployment along the Western Front. There was, however, continued inter-service rivalry with the RFC which led to wastage in aircraft and other resources. But more seriously for the politicians, the division had a big impact on the air defence of Britain itself. Neither service seemed able to combat German air attacks. It was agreed to merge the two services. On 1 April 1918 the RNAS, which at this time had 67,000 officers and men, 2,949 aircraft, 103 airships and 126 coastal stations, merged with the RFC to form the Royal Air Force. A brief history of the RNAS is at www.theaerodrome.com/services/gbritain/rnas/index.php.

Service records for other ranks in the RNAS, who did not transfer to the RAF (or who had died or been invalided out before 1 April 1918), are in ADM 188 and can be searched in the normal way (see above). Officers' records are in ADM 273. They are arranged by service number order, although there is an index available through TNA online catalogue. The records will give you details of which units an individual served with, next of kin and often candid comments by superior officers about performance and conduct. Entries will indicate whether an individual transferred to the RAF or not.

Also of use may be pieces AIR 1/2108/207/49/1 to AIR 1/2111/207/49/9, which contain detailed lists of where officers were based between 1916 and 1918. These include officers appointed for service at the Admiralty Air Department, giving the section they were attached to, officers attached to squadrons and stations, to overseas expeditionary forces, on board ships and on detached duty with other ministries. There is also a list of officers sick, missing, interned or prisoners of war. Officers are indexed alphabetically so that individuals can be found easily and their postings identified. The lists may also serve as a means of identifying RNAS units if you're struggling to identify a set of initials on a service record.

Details of the campaign medals issued to individuals are in ADM 171 (and online at Ancestry). Ancestry has also made available details of the pilots' licences awarded by the Royal Aero Club. Generally, these licences were issued before the RNAS and RFC established their own training facilities so they are most useful for the early years of flying.

If your ancestor transferred to the new service, officer's records are in AIR 76 (online through DocumentsOnline) and records for other ranks in AIR 79 (not yet online). Both these series only contain records for officers and men who left before the end of 1920, otherwise the records are still with the RAF. More details about obtaining post-1920 personnel records can be found at www.veterans-uk.info. A register of air personnel during the First World War is kept by David Barnes at www.rfc-rnas-raf-register.org.uk; there is a charge for searches.

A wide range of operational records for RNAS squadrons and bases are in series AIR 1, with some material in ADM 137. It might be helpful to know that on the establishment of the RAF existing naval air squadrons were given the prefix 2, so 1 Squadron RNAS became 201 Squadron RAF.

Useful further reading is William Spencer's *Air Force Records for Family Historians* (PRO, 2000) and Phil Tomaselli's *Tracing Your RAF Ancestors* (Pen & Sword, 2009).

Fleet Air Arm (FAA)

After years of bitter disputes the Fleet Air Arm was finally transferred from the Air Ministry to the Admiralty in 1937. In September 1939, the

A Swordfish is gently guided down onto an escort carrier, somewhere in the Atlantic.
(Crown Copyright)

Fleet Air Arm consisted of 20 squadrons and 232 aircraft on strength. The war gave a new impetus to naval flying which gradually changed naval tactics from a ship versus ship conflict to aircraft versus ships, often with devastating effects. The crippling of the Italian Fleet in Taranto harbour by Swordfish biplanes carrying torpedoes in a night attack in 1940 was undoubtedly the most notable Fleet Air Arm success of the war. However, the FAA served in almost every theatre, taking part in the Battles of France, Britain and the Atlantic, Russian convoys, the invasion of Madagascar, North African and Libyan campaigns, the invasions of Italy and Southern France, D-Day, the Pacific and the planned invasion of Japan.

The FAA was also instrumental in sinking the greatest tonnage of enemy shipping, and was one of the main weapons against the U-boat.

FAA aircrew were also adept at aerial combat and had many air aces, and received numerous honours, including two Victoria Crosses and many Distinguished Service Orders (DSO), Distinguished Service Crosses, Distinguished Service Medals (DSM) and Mentions in Despatches.

In September 1945 the strength of the Fleet Air Arm was: 59 aircraft carriers, 3,700 aircraft, 72,000 officers and men and 56 air stations all over the world. The aircraft carrier had replaced the battleship as the Fleet's capital ship and its aircraft were strike weapons in their own right.

Personnel records are with the Ministry of Defence. Combat reports compiled by pilots are in AIR 50 at Kew.

A roll of honour for FAA officers and ratings who lost their lives during the war can be found at www.fleetairarmarchive.net/RollofHonour/Index.html. The FAA Memorial Chapel is St Bartholomew's Church, Yeovilton, near the FAA Museum in Somerset.

An (incomplete) list of honours and awards made to Fleet Air Arm personnel can be found in William Chatterton Dickson's *Seedie's List of Fleet Air Arm Awards 1939–1969* (Ripley Registers, 1990). A copy is in TNA Library and can be found at other museums and large reference libraries. An online list of gallantry awards and how to find out more about them is at www.fleetairarmarchive.net.

Some FAA personnel received RAF awards and you may need to go through the records in AIR 30 at TNA.

Fleet Air Arm squadrons were assigned numbers between 700 and 899 and 1700 and 1899. Surviving Operations Record Books of Fleet Air Arm squadrons up to 1948 are in ADM 207, with a few in AIR 27, and operational records after 1948 in ADM 335. Copies of these books, together with sets of line books, which are basically more informative and personal ORBs and are particularly useful for the post-war period, and much other information about individual squadrons (and indeed individual members of the Arm and the aircraft they flew) can be found at the Fleet Air Arm Museum's Centre for Naval Aviation Records and Research.

Reports of Proceedings about missions and operations compiled by commanding officers are with those of ships and squadrons in ADM 199 and elsewhere. As the FAA worked closely with RAF Coastal Command, it may be worth checking headquarters papers for the Command in AIR 15 and Operations Record Books in AIR 24.

No aircraft carrier flying log books are known to have survived.

A superb website is the Fleet Air Arm Archive at www.fleet airarmarchive.net, although it has not been updated for a few years. On it you can a find a roll of honour, lists of FAA prisoners of war, histories of squadrons, job descriptions for the technical and support staff and biographies of notable pilots. The Sea Your History website also has some useful pages at www.seayourhistory.org.uk/content/view/454/613/.

Two informative books are John Winton's *Find, Fix and Strike! – The FAA at War 1939–45* (BT Batsford, 1980) and Ray Sturtivant and Theo Balance's *The Squadrons of the Fleet Air Arm* (Air Britain (Historians) Ltd, 1994) which provides a brief history for each FAA Squadron, listing aircraft types flown, where based and commanding officers.

The Fleet Air Arm Museum at Yeovilton is a superb museum on the theme of naval aviation and is well worth visiting. Details are given in Appendix 5.

Women's Royal Naval Service (WRNS)

Before the First World War, women, apart from a few nurses, were excluded from service in either the Army or the Navy. And despite an outburst of patriotic fervour during the early weeks of the war by women, this was the position until 1916, when an increasing shortage of men and

A service record for Emily Skilton who served with the WRNS as a steward in 1918. (TNA ADM 336/24)

the desire to release men from clerical and support roles so they could go to the front line led the authorities to begin to change their mind. The Royal Navy in 1916 was the first service to recruit women to take over the role of cooks, clerks, wireless telegraphists, code experts and electricians, although it took until November 1917 to set up the Women's Royal Naval Service (WRNS). However, only just over 5,000 women served in the service, of whom 23 lost their lives. Two series of records exist for the WRNS, both found at TNA. Service registers for the 438 officers are in series ADM 321 and a selection of personal files in ADM 318. Records for ratings are in ADM 336. They are arranged in service-number order, with an alphabetical index to names. ADM 318 and ADM 336 are available through DocumentsOnline. Medal rolls are in ADM 171/93 (and on Ancestry). The WRNS was disbanded in 1919. A history of the WRNS in the First World War can be found at www.seayourhistory.org.uk.

In April 1939, with the threat of another war looming over Europe, the Royal Navy re-established the Women's Royal Naval Service. The new service gave its recruits far greater levels of responsibility than their mothers had had a generation earlier, with an ever-expanding range of duties. Many members saw active service during the war, and over 100 lost their lives.

Applicants had to be aged between 18 and 45 (later amended to between 17½ and 50), and to be British subjects of British descent. Exacting standards were expected, and this perhaps led to the WRNS's reputation for favouring women with middle-class backgrounds, although in practice they came from all social classes. At its peak in September 1944, the Women's Royal Naval Service numbered 74,620 officers and ratings, in 90 categories and in 50 branches, with women doing over 200 different jobs.

Initially, women were recruited for office-based or domestic duties, but as the war progressed they were gradually deployed to more demanding and dangerous tasks, including code-breaking, signalling, bomb range-marking, radar detecting, air mechanics and as coxswains of smaller boats on D-Day.

Wrens were not subjected to the same disciplinary regulations as their male counterparts, as they were still technically civilians. Each naval base had a Port Superintendent, who was not only responsible for the recruitment of WRNS personnel, but also for ensuring high standards of competence and behaviour. Salaries were fairly low, but board and lodging were provided, so most Wrens were able to at least maintain a comfortable standard of living.

Resentment from the regular troops as women increasingly took over traditional male roles was an inescapable part of a Wren's working life, but WRNS personnel quickly established their worth, earning widespread admiration and respect for their willingness to undertake any work allotted to them.

As the war progressed, women were increasingly sent to bases abroad, and were eventually spread throughout South Africa, North and East Africa, the Americas, North West Europe, India, Australia, the Persian Gulf and the Mediterranean. Overseas postings could last up to two-and-a-half years.

Despite the WRNS's motto 'Never at Sea', some women did get a taste of life on board. This involved anything from making deliveries and assisting with naval training exercises to helping tow stricken boats back to Britain after the Normandy invasions of June 1944.

Shortly after the declaration of peace in the summer of 1945, demobilisation began. The role played by the WRNS had been crucial, and in October 1945 Vera Laughton Matthews, the WRNS Director, told the recruits: 'The war is over and you have had a hand in winning it. You have helped to lift this burden of horror and suffering from the world.'

The WRNS remained in existence after the war, and was declared a Permanent Service in 1949. In 1990 women were officially deployed at sea for the first time, and three years later were fully integrated into the Royal Navy.

Service records for WRNS after 1919 are with the Directorate of Personnel Support (Navy), Navy Search, TNT Archive Services, Tetron Point, William Nadin Way, Swadlincote DE11 0BB. There is likely to be a charge of £30 for supplying records except to the next of kin. Series ADM 199 and ADM 116 contain much about the Royal Navy in the Second World War and include references to the WRNS.

The Royal Naval Museum in Portsmouth has a large collection of documents and photographs. The museum's Sea Your History website (www.seayourhistory.org.uk) features an extensive history of the WRNS, and includes links to the stories of individual Wrens, all of which give a fascinating insight into their lives and the work they undertook.

The Imperial War Museum also has material relating to the WRNS, including film, video and sound archives, journals and cuttings, books, photographs and the private papers of individuals. Small collections are also with the Second World War Experience Centre in Yorkshire.

The Commonwealth War Graves Commission has records of female casualties of both world wars, including those Wrens who lost their lives on active service.

Several excellent pages on Wren's experiences can be found at www.war-experience.org/history/keyaspects/wrns/default.asp and to a lesser extent on the Association of Wrens website at www.wrens.org.uk.

The story of the WRNS is told in Marjorie H. Fletcher's *The WRNS, A History of the Women's Royal Naval Service* (Naval Institute Press, 1989). Also of interest is Eileen Bigland's *The Story of the WRNS* (Nicolson and Watson, 1946).

Chapter 6

AUXILIARY FORCES AND THE COASTGUARD

Since the mid-nineteenth century the Navy has supported a number of auxiliary forces, which have allowed the Navy to maintain a trained reserve of men who can be called upon in times of war. Most, but not all, of these men were already employed on merchant ships so there may be other records about them (see Appendix 3). There were two main branches: the Royal Naval Reserve (recruited from merchant seamen) and the larger Royal Naval Volunteer Reserve (who came from amateur seamen and the wider general public). They were merged in 1958 as the Royal Naval Reserve.

Lt Nicholas Monsarrat, RNVR who was an officer aboard several corvettes during the Second World War and eventually commanded a frigate. (Lt Cdr R. F. J. Maberley, RNVR)

Royal Naval Reserve (RNR)

The Reserve was established in 1859 as a reserve force of officers and men from deep-sea merchant ships and fishing vessels. At the outbreak of the First World War it had a strength of around 30,000 men. During the two world wars men served with distinction on all the ships maintained by the Royal Navy. A few men also qualified as pilots and flew with the Royal Navy Aerial Service and Fleet Air Arm (see p. 108).

The service record for Thomas James Fowler who served in the Royal Naval Reserve. (TNA BT 164/21)

Officers

Officers are listed in the Navy List from 1862. Information given includes name, rank, date of commission and seniority, as well as the ships on which the officers served.

Service records for officers who served between 1862 and 1920 are in ADM 240. They are arranged by rank and seniority and show details of merchant as well as naval service and are arranged in numerical order of commission. There are no separate indexes but some of the pieces contain indexes. Additional information can often be found in the service cards and files in ADM 340, which in a few cases go up to the Second World War.

The Fleet Air Arm Museum also holds record cards for RNR officers, including Executive (X); Engineers (E); Cadets; and Warrant Officer Telegraphic. In addition, the Museum has nearly one-hundred pay and appointing ledgers for officers of the RNR (as well as those in the RNVR) for the First World War, which can offer useful information on pay movements (including tax bills and probate) to complement the officers' records at Kew.

Ratings

The Fleet Air Arm Museum holds original records for RNR ratings from 1908 to 1955 (see Appendix 5). A representative sample of records for men who served in the RNR between 1860 and 1913 is in BT 164 at Kew. These consist of volumes and cards, each page or card representing five years' service in the Reserve. The entries are in numerical order of enrolment. The records are available on DocumentsOnline. Records of RNR Ratings between 1914 and 1919 are available on microfiche in series BT 377.

In 1914, a Shetland Royal Naval Reserve was formed on the Shetlands. Unlike the regular RNR, it was a coast-watching and local defence organisation. It was disbanded in 1921. Records for ratings are in piece BT 377/7. They can be easily identified as the letter L prefixes their service numbers.

During the First World War there was a Mercantile Marine Reserve (MMR) made up of merchant seamen serving on merchant vessels requisitioned by the Admiralty for wartime service. Some of these men may have been members of the Royal Naval Reserve with records in BT 377 and they would have eligible for the Mercantile Marine Medal, for which there is a medal roll in BT 351 (and on DocumentsOnline).

Royal Naval Volunteer Reserve (RNVR)

The Royal Naval Volunteer Reserve (RNVR), founded in 1903, was a force of officers and ratings who undertook naval training in their spare time, but who were not professional seamen. In 1936, a Royal Naval Volunteer Supplementary Reserve was formed to attract yachtsmen. During both world wars the RNVR was the principal means by which officers could enter the Royal Navy for the duration of the war. The service was colloquially called the 'Wavy Navy', after the distinctive wavy rings RNVR officers wore on their sleeves to differentiate them from RN/RNR officers. An interesting memoir of life in the RNVR is at www.swmaritime.org.uk/articles.php?atype=a.

The service record for Thomas Fowler who was killed on HMS Indefatigable *during the Battle of Jutland.* (TNA ADM 337/38)

Officers

Officers are listed in the *Navy Lists*. Service records of RNVR officers can be found in two series: ADM 337 and ADM 340. Records in ADM 337/117-128 cover the period up to 1922 and can be downloaded from DocumentsOnline. These pieces are also searchable by name on TNA catalogue. The records in ADM 340, which generally cover the inter-war and Second World War periods, include files and record-of-service cards detailing the service of RNVR officers.

Ratings

Service records for ratings are in ADM 337/1-108 (and on Documents Online). Details of medals awarded for service in the First World War are in ADM 171/125-129. The RNVR was initially divided into divisions, each of which had its own distinguishing letter, that is a letter placed before the service number of its men, so the service number may indicate both the division and the company to which a man belonged, such as E for Birmingham Electrical Volunteers. These numbers are listed in the In-depth Research Guide on the RNVR found on TNA website.

Royal Fleet Auxiliary (RFA)

The RFA was first established in 1905 to provide coaling ships for the Navy and now replenishes and resupplies Royal Navy vessels around the world. During the Second World War the RFA came into its own when the British Fleet was often far from home. After 1945, the RFA has supported the operations of the Royal Navy in the many conflicts in which it has been involved in, particularly the Falklands War in 1982 (where one vessel was lost and another badly damaged).

Until 1921, the officers of the Royal Fleet Auxiliaries were nearly all RNR officers and ranked accordingly. Since then they have been ranked as Merchant Navy officers.

The Fleet Air Arm Museum holds the crew books for Royal Fleet Auxiliary and Mercantile Fleet Auxiliary (MFA) for the First World War. These contain alphabetical indexes of ships, crew lists (entries and discharges), rates of pay, next of kin, etc. See Appendix 2 for more details.

The RFA Historical Society maintains an excellent website devoted to the Auxiliary's history at www.historicalrfa.org with a roll of honour and descriptions of ships in the RFA. In addition, the Royal Fleet Auxiliary

Association Archive has a small collection of several thousand photographs, documents, ephemera and artefacts at 3–4 Station House, Bellingham, Hexham NE48 2DG; www.rfa-association.org/cms/index.php. It is open by appointment only.

Royal Naval Reserve Trawler Section (RNR(T))

The RNR was generally confined to officers and men of deep-sea merchantmen but in 1911 it was felt that there was a need to employ trawlers in wartime as minesweepers and patrol vessels. The Royal Naval Reserve Trawler Section was set up to enrol the necessary personnel. Although abolished as a separate section of the RNR in 1921, the RNR(T) always remained quite distinct from the RNR proper.

Service records of ratings who served in the RNR(T) can be found in BT 377. Their service numbers were prefixed with the letters DA, ES, SA, SB or TS. The records of ratings whose service numbers begin with SBC have not survived.

Royal Naval Patrol Service

During the Second World War the Royal Naval Patrol Service ('Harry Tate's Navy') recruited largely from fishermen who manned small vessels such as minesweepers. It very much regarded itself as being a Navy within a Navy with a strong camaraderie. At its peak, there were some 70,000 members serving on 6,000 vessels. There are two informative websites devoted to the Patrol Service: www.harry-tates.org.uk and www.rnps.lowestoft.org.uk. An interesting site detailing specific individuals' wartime service with the RNR and RNPS is at www.royal-naval-reserve.co.uk/research.htm. There is a small museum dedicated to the service at their wartime headquarters, Sparrow's Nest (HMS *Europa*) in Lowestoft.

Royal Naval Division (RND)

In the early months of the war the Navy had a surplus of 30,000 men. In response, the First Sea Lord, Winston Churchill, organised several brigades of the Naval Division, who fought alongside the Army, initially defending Antwerp then later at Gallipoli and in Flanders. In 1916, the Division was transferred to the Army as 63rd (Royal Naval) Division. Despite the fact that the Division was operating in conditions very different from the high seas, naval discipline was maintained. Time continued to be regulated by bells as if aboard ship. Men referred to leaving the front line as 'going ashore'. There was also a long-running battle over the wearing of beards, which were prohibited in the Army, but allowed in the Navy. Indeed, the brigades themselves were named after naval heroes: Anson, Benbow (disbanded in 1916), Collingwood (disbanded in 1916), Drake, Hawke, Hood, Howe and Nelson.

Service records for officers in the Royal Naval Division (RND) are in ADM 339/3, with the equivalent for ratings in ADM 339/1, although records of ratings who died on active service are in ADM 339/2. They are available through DocumentsOnline. War diaries for the brigades into which the Division was divided are in WO 95 (many of which can also be downloaded from DocumentsOnline) and ADM 137. There are databases to deaths of men in the RND online at Ancestry and Findmypast. In addition, www.royalnavaldivision.co.uk tells the story of a few of the men in the Division and gives some points on research. The memoirs of Able Seaman James Hart, who served with the Benbow Battalion at Gallipoli, are online at http://benbowbattalion1915.co.uk.

A number of naval brigades were assembled during the late nineteenth century, made up of seamen and marines who fought alongside the Army in a variety of colonial wars, notably the Boer War. That your ancestor was a member of one of these brigades should be clear from his service papers. Medal rolls listing all participants are in ADM 171 (and online on Ancestry) and there may be the occasional file detailing their exploits elsewhere in the Admiralty series. Descriptions of the campaigns they took part in can be found in Arthur Bleby's *Victorian Naval Brigades* (Whittles, 2006), and Wikipedia also has a useful summary of the actions in which they took part. More information can be found in a Royal Naval Museum leaflet at http://tinyurl.com/6gdmp68.

Service Records Not Yet Transferred to TNA

Service records for members of the RNR who served between 1929 and 1950 are with: Navy Search, TNT Archives Services, Textron Point, William Nadine Way, Swadlincote DE 11 0PB; email: navysearch@pgrc. tnt.co.uk. This is also the address to contact for officers and ratings who served in the RNVR between 1920 (1923 for officers) and 1958.

For records of RNR officers who served after 1950 and ratings (from 1945) contact: PPPA (Pay, Pensions, Personnel, Administration), Centurion Building, Grange Road, Gosport PO13 9XA. In both cases, a charge in the region of £30 is likely to be made.

HM Coastguard

The Coastguard was not of course an auxiliary service, but there always has been a close link between it and the Royal Navy. This is in part because the Navy used the Coastguard as an unofficial auxiliary force during at least part of the nineteenth century, and the majority of coastguards have served in the Navy.

Traditionally, the Coastguard had three roles: preventing smuggling, defending the coastline in time of war and rescuing ships and seamen in distress. The first coastguards were appointed at the end of the seventeenth century by the Board of Customs. In 1809, the government established a Preventive Water Guard to tackle smugglers close to shore, which was merged with two other similar services to form HM Coastguard. In 1831, the service employed nearly 6,700 men. In 1856, after the Crimean War – during which the Coastguard first functioned as a reserve force for the Royal Navy – control was transferred to the Admiralty from the Board of Customs.

The Coastguard as run by the Admiralty consisted of three distinct bodies: the Shore Force, the Permanent Cruiser Force and Guard Ships, naval ships that lay at major ports to act as headquarters of Coastguard districts. In 1923, responsibility passed to the Board of Trade.

A coastguard station crew in the early 1890s. The exact location is not known. (Frank Bowen, *His Majesty's Coastguard* (Hutchinson, 1928))

Because of the confused administrative history of the Coastguard there are a number of sources. Only the most important are listed here. A comprehensive list can be found in the In-depth Research Guide *Coastguard*.

Service records between roughly 1822 and 1923 are in ADM 175. Unfortunately, there is no index, so you have to know roughly when and where your ancestor served. It does not help that between 1866 and 1886 there is an unexplained gap in the records. It is possible that this series of records will be digitised and fully indexed within a few years. In the meantime, if you have a fast broadband connection you can download individual pieces from this series through the DocumentsOnline Digital Microfilm service free of charge. TNA's idea is to encourage users to index the records for themselves, but as far as I am aware nobody has yet done so.

During the First World War many men were awarded campaign medals, which are listed in the naval medal rolls in ADM 171 (and on Ancestry). Unfortunately, their bravery did not prevent a reduction on the size of the service and many men were made redundant in government cuts in the early 1920s. Details of the men who lost their jobs are also in ADM 175.

Coastguards' pensions paid by the Admiralty between 1866 and 1926 are recorded in ADM 23. Other pensions between 1855 and 1935 were paid by the Paymaster General and can be found in PMG 23 and in PMG 70. Coastguard officers appear in the *Navy Lists*.

Further Reading

TNA has In-depth Research Guides to the records of the Royal Naval Reserve and Royal Naval Volunteer Reserve, which is supplemented by an excellent, if idiosyncratic, introduction to the somewhat tangled network of naval volunteer units by Len Barnett at www.barnettmaritime.co.uk/reserves.htm#mmr. A recent history is Stephen Howarth's *The Royal Navy' Reserves in War and Peace 1903–2003* (Leo Cooper, 2003).

'Your Archives' (http://yourarchives.nationalarchives.gov.uk), the Wiki formerly maintained by TNA, also has an interesting history of the Coastguard and some other finding aids. In addition, the Society of Genealogists has the late Eileen Stage's incomplete index to individual coastguards. Details of the Society are in Appendix 5. A useful history of the Coastguard is Graham Smith's *Something to Declare! 1,000 Years of*

Customs and Excise (Harrap, 1980). More about the history of the Coastguard can be found at www.hansonclan.co.uk/coastguards_1.htm and on the Maritime and Coastguard Agency (which is responsible for the Coastguard today) website at http://tinyurl.com/3xg5dc6.

Chapter 7

CARE OF THE SICK AND WOUNDED

The Royal Navy, the Admiralty and, during the eighteenth century, the Sick and Hurt Board have always been deeply concerned about the health of seamen. Not only, perhaps not principally, on humanitarian grounds, but because of the practical problems of manning ships. Trained seamen, sick or, even worse, dead men were very difficult to replace. So real efforts were made to prevent that loss and the disease that caused it, as well as to provide a basic level of care as understood at

A Royal Navy surgeon with his family in an early carte de visite. (Richard Taylor)

the time. If you've been on a tour of HMS *Victory* you may remember the sick bay and, in particular, the cramped area assigned the surgeon and his team during battle.

Until the twentieth century, medical care was generally better than that offered to soldiers in the field and probably as good as that available to the average civilian. The Navy was also reasonably progressive in introducing new medical innovations. The Sick and Hurt Board (before its abolition in 1806) in particular was keen to experiment with ways to improve sailors' health. The smallpox vaccination was adopted within a few years of its development, although it was slow to introduce measures to tackle scurvy (a disease caused by a lack of vitamin C), which was a major problem at sea. More recently, Britain's first blood bank was set up at Haslar Hospital in Gosport, which was the main naval hospital, in 1940.

Each ship had a surgeon and an assistant or two (sometimes called mates) who patched up sailors who were wounded in battle or had been the victim of an accident, such as falling from the rigging, or were suffering from disease: dysentery and rheumatism being particularly common.

Surgery was rudimentary, and few effective medicines were available. Until 1804, surgeons were expected to provide their own drugs and equipment. Most surgeons took pride in the speed with which they could perform an amputation, which was vital to reduce the effects of shock. Significant improvements in skills and the quality of treatment, though, had to wait until anaesthesia began to be used after 1846 and an effective antiseptic became available after 1865. Amputation was then the only treatment considered for limbs smashed by splinters or cannon balls. In the midst of a battle the loblolly men, semi-trained able seamen (not the surgeons' assistants, who were more skilled), could easily fill a tub with severed limbs, which would be thrown overboard at midnight every day along with the bodies of the deceased. Complicated surgical procedures on abdominal wounds were impossible, even on shore, until well into the nineteenth century. Infections were almost inevitable. And these sorts of wound were often fatal. Samuel Leech, who was able seaman on board HMS *Macedonian* during an engagement with the USS *United States* in 1812, wrote in his memoirs:

Among the wounded was a brave fellow named Wells. After the surgeon had amputated and dressed his arm, he walked about in fine spirits, as if he had received only a slight injury. Indeed, while under the operation, he manifested a similar heroism – observing to the surgeon, 'I have lost my arm in the service of my country; but I don't mind it, doctor, it's the fortune of war.' Cheerful and gay as he was, he soon died. His companions gave him rum; he was attacked by fever and died. Thus his messmates actually killed him with kindness.

Until well into the nineteenth century the medical training of surgeons was minimal and their reputation was not always high. Ordinary seaman Aaron Thomas writing in 1795 considered surgeons lazy and drunken: 'the business being entirely conducted by surgeon's mates. The surgeons rarely know more of the men's diseases than they take from the sick list or the verbal word of their mates …'. Lieutenant Wybourn of the Royal Marines, who fell very ill when stationed at Naples, reported to his sister that: 'the surgeon is such a brute that had I not had more fortitude than many, [he] would have hastened my end … To the skill and attention of the Mate, a very attractive young man, I may attribute my recovery.' Yet their skills gradually improved and for nearly fifty years, naval surgeons sailed on board emigrant ships where they were responsible for the health of the passengers and ensuring that the ship itself was clean and wholesome.

Matters increasingly improved during the nineteenth century. Despite the lack of anaesthesia and antiseptics, the standard of surgery in the service in the early nineteenth century was generally good. During a voyage surgeons had to undertake various roles as physician, apothecary and health advisor for the crew, although the range of their medical work was inevitably more narrow than that experienced by their professional brethren in civil life. Naval surgeons cared predominantly for wounds and injuries, venereal afflictions and epidemic diseases, such as typhus, typhoid or yellow fever in the crowded environment of vessels and in tropical climates. Untreated injuries often caused contamination. The Royal Navy recruited young men trained and examined in medicine, and then sent them out to start their careers either for a few years at one of the large naval hospitals at Portsmouth or Plymouth or else directly to sick bays aboard ships where they worked alongside the loblolly boys who served as nursing staff.

Researching Naval Surgeons

The term 'surgeon' traditionally described a person who performed operations with the use of surgical instruments. Many records are held by the Royal College of Surgeons of England, 35–43 Lincoln's Inn Fields, London WC2A 3PE; www.rcseng.ac.uk, including examinations of surgeons before they joined the Navy between 1745 and 1800. Other records between 1700 and 1800 are in ADM 106/2952-2963. However, as many naval surgeons were Scottish or Irish, you may need to contact the Royal College of Physicians and Surgeons of Glasgow, 234–42 St Vincent Street, Glasgow; www.rcpsg.ac.uk, the Royal College of Surgeons of Edinburgh, Nicolson Street, Edinburgh EH8 9W; www.library.rcsed.ac.uk, or the Royal College of Surgeons in Ireland, 123 St Stephens Green, Dublin 2; www.rcsi.ie.

Details of surgeons practising since 1845 can be found in published medical directories and medical registers, and surgeons and other medical officers serving in the Navy are of course in the *Navy Lists*. There are also professional journals which may give you details of a man's career and an obituary at the end of it, such as this entry from the *Medical Times and Gazette* for 13 July 1861 (the magazine is available on Google Books): 'July 3rd 1861 death – Swann July 3, at Weedon, Northamptonshire, Edward Swann, late Staff Surgeon to the Military District prison, at Weedon, formerly Assistant Surgeon in the Royal Navy, and afterwards Ordnance Surgeon, aged 83. The deceased gentleman served in the Walcheren Expedition, and the siege of Flushing.' Swann would have had his work cut out at Walcheren which was arguably the worst British military disaster during the Napoleonic Wars. It was a joint operation by the Royal Navy and British Army during the summer of 1809 to capture the Dutch island of Walcheren at the mouth of the Scheldt. It was dreadfully planned and executed, with thousands of soldiers and sailors being affected by a mysterious rheumatic fever which killed thousands and debilitated the rest. More about researching Edward Swann's career can be found at http://richardramsayarmstrong. blogspot.com.

TNA also has a number of records for surgeons. Lists of surgeons for various dates are in ADM 11/40, 70-72, with service records between 1774 and 1904 in ADM 104 and ADM 6/443-444. Similar records for assistant surgeons from 1795 to 1903 are also in ADM 104. Details of pensions paid to surgeons and related positions between 1805 and 1875 are in ADM 104/66.

Peter Davis has an excellent website at www.pdavis.nl devoted to his ancestor William Loney, who was a naval surgeon between 1839 and 1877, with a lot about the man and a large amount of background about naval surgeons of the time.

Medical Officers' Journals

Some of the most interesting naval records are the medical officers' journals and diaries in ADM 101, which were compiled by Royal Navy surgeons and assistant surgeons serving on HM ships, hospitals, naval brigades, shore parties and on emigrant and convict ships. These officers were required to submit detailed records of the health and treatment of those under their care in the form of journals. They are probably the most significant collection of records for the study of health and medicine at sea for the nineteenth century. Individual journals include a variety of colourful tales of eighteenth- and nineteenth-century ship life, from drunken rum-related incidents, venereal disease, scurvy, shark bites and tarantulas to lightning strikes, gun fights, mutiny, arrests and courts martial – not to mention shipwrecks and even murder.

TNA has recently catalogued the journals between 1793 and 1880 (they actually go up to 1963) and the results can be found in the online catalogue. Examples of some of the registers and additional information are at www.nationalarchives.gov.uk/surgeonsatsea.

The journals often mention the men who were being treated for wounds or other ailments. For example, in the journal kept by William Beatty, the surgeon on HMS *Victory* for early November 1805, the following names are mentioned:

> Joseph Connell, able seaman; nature of wound or contusion, wounded face; cured on board, sent to hospital or died, 1 November; William Welsh, landsman; nature of wound or contusion, wounded arm; cured on board, sent to hospital or died, 1 November; William Mainland, ordinary seaman; nature of wound or contusion, wounded face slightly; cured on board, sent to hospital or died, 4 November. (ADM 101/125/1, f. 38)

Curiously, there is no mention of any treatment for the fatal wounds incurred by Lord Nelson. If they lived the men would have been sent to the naval hospital in Gibraltar (and they should appear in the hospital musters in ADM 102/231).

Unfortunately, almost all journals later than about 1919 remain closed to public access, in compliance with data-protection legislation. However, some twentieth-century journals that were not selected for preservation at TNA are now with the Admiralty Library in Portsmouth.

Nurses

Nursing care on board naval vessels and in many hospitals on land was the responsibility of male sick-bay attendants, who received special training but otherwise should be researched in the same way as ordinary ratings. They were first appointed in 1833, and a separate branch was created in 1884. Female sick-berth attendants were first appointed in 1949. They replaced loblolly boys, said to be so named after the porridge they brought to the sick. They were seamen and marines who drifted towards this work – or were detailed to do it.

On land the position was very different. Initially, the sick at Haslar and Plymouth were cared for by the widows of sailors and marines or by old pensioners who happened to live nearby. Many of the women were of 'ill repute', often drunk and frequently thieves. The position was finally resolved after the Napoleonic Wars when nursing in naval hospitals was undertaken by men, usually ex-seamen or marines, who were recruited as required from the shore establishments and who had no nursing

A seaman's wife tends a mortally wounded sailor. (William Glasscock, *Naval Sketch Book* (1835))

qualifications. A few female nurses were also employed and a number of widows and wives of naval ratings were taken on to care for the old seamen in Royal Greenwich Hospital.

However, by the 1880s this state of affairs was increasingly unsatisfactory at a time when nursing and medical science in general was becoming much more professional. An Admiralty committee recommended in 1884 the appointment of trained male sick-berth staff and female nurses. A female nursing service was established initially at the main hospitals at Haslar and Plymouth, and was extended in 1897 to Chatham and Malta, and in 1901 to all Royal Navy hospitals. The names of matrons and head sisters first appear in the *Navy List* of 1884.

In the wards the sisters were addressed as 'Madam' by both staff and patients and absurd precautions were taken to protect them from the discomfort of viewing any part of the patients' bodies other than the head, shoulders and feet. An important part of the sisters' responsibilities was the practical instruction of the newly formed sick-berth staff. The sisters originally wore a uniform of a navy-blue serge dress, white apron, small navy-blue serge shoulder capes and white frilled caps with strings. In the summer this was replaced by a white blouse and blue skirt.

In 1902, the Naval Nursing Services received Royal approval and the title of the service changed to Queen Alexandra's Royal Naval Nursing Service. A QARNNS' Reserve, of civilian nurses, for service in wartime only was also set up.

The Records

Most records are at TNA and more details are given in the In-depth Research Guide *Nurses and Nursing Services: Royal Navy*. Registers of nurses employed at the Royal Greenwich Hospital between 1704 and 1865 are in ADM 73/83-88. Of particular interest is piece ADM 73/85 which includes details of the nurse's husband's naval service and any children between 1783 and 1863. Applications from ratings' widows applying for admission to Royal Greenwich Hospital as nurses between 1817 and 1842 are in ADM 6/329 and ADM 6/331. There are various records for female nurses who joined between 1884 and the late 1920s in ADM 104, including registers and service records in ADM 104/43, 95, 96 and 161. Details of nurses in the QARNNS' Reserves, who signed up for wartime service only during the First World War, are in ADM 104/ 162–165.

An Edwardian wood cut of the cockpit on the Victory. *In cramped conditions such as these surgeons and their teams operated in the midst of battle.* (Henry J. Sparks, *The Story of Portsmouth* (Portsmouth, 1921))

Records from the late 1920s to the present day are with the Directorate of Personnel Support (Navy), Navy Search, TNT Archive Services, Tetron Point, William Nadin Way, Swadlincote DE11 0BB. A charge may be made for copies of records. A little more about the service and its history can be found at www.qarnns.co.uk.

Naval nurses were also eligible for the Royal Red Cross, which was established in 1883 for ladies who showed special devotion while nursing the sick and wounded of the Army and Navy. The registers are in WO 145, although they contain very little about why the medal was awarded, and recipients are also listed in the *London Gazette*.

Hospitals

From the mid-eighteenth century the Navy built a number of hospitals at its bases around the world. The first was actually at Port Mahon in Menorca in 1713. The first in Britain was at Haslar near Gosport, which took patients from 1753. Other large hospitals were at Plymouth, Chatham, Malta and Gibraltar.

Records are largely at TNA, although staff and some other records for the Plymouth Naval Hospital at East Stonehouse, which was open between 1756 and 1995, are at the Plymouth and West Devon Archives Centre (www.plymouth.gov.uk/archives) and a few records of the Naval Hospital, which looked after the mentally ill, in Great Yarmouth (including staff books) are with the National Maritime Museum. Unfortunately, few if any records appear to survive for the hospital in Chatham.

There are a number of series at Kew that might be of use if you are researching staff or patients, including:

- ADM 101 – the index to medical officers' journals on TNA's catalogue often mention that individual patients have been sent to particular naval hospitals.
- ADM 102 – musters for hospitals, which record the names of patients, the reason for their admission and when they were discharged either cured or, too often, deceased. The records run between 1756 and 1926 and are arranged by hospital or hospital ship. Also included are many pay lists for staff at these hospitals.
- ADM 104 – mainly contains lists and papers about medical staff, particularly surgeons and nurses.
- ADM 105 – contains some reports made on hospitals after visits by senior naval personnel.
- ADM 304 – records of the naval hospital at Valetta in Malta.

There may also be correspondence in series ADM 1 and ADM 116 about individual hospitals, although patients and staff are unlikely to be mentioned. Surviving minutes of the Sick and Hurt Board (officially known as Commissioners of Sick and Wounded Seamen) are in ADM 99 with correspondence in ADM 97 and ADM 98. Some correspondence and other papers are also at the National Maritime Museum. The Board was abolished in 1806 and its duties taken over by the Transport Board. In turn, the Transport Board was eventually absorbed into the Navy Board, which became part of the Admiralty in 1832.

An interesting article on medical health in the eighteenth century is P. K. Crimmin's 'The Sick and Hurt Board and the health of seamen c. 1700–1806', *Journal for Maritime Research* (1999); www.jmr.nmm.ac.uk/ server/show/ConJmrArticle.12/setPaginate/No. The main history remains J. J. Keevil, J. L. S. Coulter and C. C. Lloyd's *Medicine and the Navy 1200–1900* (4 vols, Livingstone, 1957–66). Vol. One, covering the period to 1649, can be downloaded free of charge at http://world-of-books.com/?id=Jk1sAAAAMAAJ.

Haslar Hospital

The largest and most important naval hospital was at Haslar, which lies across Portsmouth harbour in Gosport. The site was an unusual location for a hospital because it was surrounded by Gosport Creek with no readily available access. It was chosen to prevent sailors from absconding. Designed by Theodore Jacobsen FRS in the manner of his Foundling Hospital in London, the hospital, reputed at one time to be the largest red-brick building in Europe, was completed in 1762, although the first patients were admitted as early as 1753. Haslar was grand in concept, elegant in design and robust of build, and provided medical attention and nursing care to the sick and wounded of both the Navy and the Army.

It may have looked very attractive but when the hospital first opened, some compared it to a prison. There were overcrowded buildings, discharged patients taking up residence in the attics and reports of drunkenness and petty theft among staff and patients. Drunkenness among the nurses, both male and female, was rife. It is perhaps little surprise that many attempts to abscond were made: in 1755 alone there were twenty-five successful escapes through the sewers.

Medical treatment may not have been of the highest order in the early years, but the standards achieved during the Peninsular and Crimean Wars earned the hospital a reputation among military authorities that was unequalled. Sir John Richardson, the eminent Arctic explorer and physician at Haslar, even corresponded with Florence Nightingale when the nursing reformer was campaigning for changes in the way casualties of war were treated.

A short history of the Hospital and interviews with some of the patients and staff can be found on the BBC webpage at http://tinyurl.com/269h6wn. Eric Birbeck's *The Royal Hospital Haslar: A Pictorial History* (Phillimore, 2009) is a recent history. TNA has some records in series ADM 305, and registers of births, marriages and deaths are in ADM 338. Muster rolls of patients between 1792 and 1854 together with pay lists of staff are in ADM 102.

During 2010 the burial ground, which may have the greatest concentration of military burials in Britain with over 7,500 known burials, was investigated by Channel 4's *Time Team* programme. At the time of writing, the programme could still be downloaded – details at www.channel4.com/programmes/time-team-specials/episode-guide/series-5/episode-2.

Lunatics

Unlike the Army, the Royal Navy tried to take special care of the men who became mentally ill as the result of their service. Many of these unfortunates probably suffered from what would today be diagnosed as shell shock or post-traumatic stress disorders. There are several musters of lunatics at Hoxton House (which was one of a complex of lunatic asylums in North London) between 1755 and 1818, when it closed (ADM 102/415-420), and at Haslar, from 1818 to 1854 (ADM 102/356-373). Yarmouth too was a major hospital for naval lunatics and there are some musters at ADM 102/825-834 (1789–1814). Other reports on the treatment of naval lunatics, between 1812 and 1832, are in ADM 105/28.

Chapter 8

THE ROYAL MARINES

The Royal Marines were first established in 1755, although they can trace their history back to 1664 as soldiers recruited to serve at sea. Traditionally, small companies of marines were responsible for maintaining discipline on board ship and participated in raiding parties on enemy ships and on land. During the nineteenth century they also took responsibility for manning the rear gun turrets on battleships and cruisers. Their modern Commando role came about during the Second World War.

The Royal Marines have long been divided into divisions at Chatham, Portsmouth and Plymouth, and from 1805 to 1869 there was also a division at Woolwich. As so many records are now online, the requirement to need to know which division a marine served with is perhaps no longer as important as it was, but it is still useful. A separate Royal Marine Artillery was formed in 1804 and a Royal Marine Light Infantry in 1855: they were merged in 1923 to form the Corps of the Royal Marines.

Officers

No original records of service of officers appointed before 1793 have survived. However, confirmation of a commission or an appointment can sometimes be found from documents or official publications of a later date. The *London Gazette* lists all commissions, promotions and resignations, as do the *Army* and *Navy Lists*. Charles Dalton's *English Army Lists and Commission Registers, 1661–1714* (6 vols, Eyre & Spottiswood, 1892) also lists many of the earliest marine officers.

The Commissions and Appointments Registers for 1703–13 and 1755–1814 (ADM 6/405-406) have brief statements about an officer's appointment. Royal Warrants for Commissions (1664–1782) are in SP 44/164-196, which are continued from 1782 in series HO 51.

Outlines of officers' careers prior to 1793 can often be reconstructed from the information given about marines officers on full pay and on half pay in the *Army List* from 1740 onwards. A set of *Army Lists* is in the Open

Reading Room at Kew. Seniority lists from 1757 to 1886 may also be useful as they give the date of promotion to a particular rank. Copies are in ADM 118/230-336 (1757–1850, indexed from 1770) and ADM 192 (1760–1886). Two surveys were carried out in 1822 and 1831 of Royal Marine officers' ages. For each officer it contains the following information: name, rank, date of seniority, actual age on 1 April 1822, whether in receipt of allowances other than pay and amount of pay. The results are in ADM 6.

Details of officers commissioned after 1793 are in Records of Officers' Services in ADM 196, which are online at DocumentsOnline. However, records are complete only from about 1837, although they go up to the 1960s.

Enquiries about officers who received their commissions after 1925 should be addressed to DPS(N)2, Building 1/152, Victory View, PP36, HMNB Portsmouth PO1 3PX.

Only three volumes of marine warrant officers' service records are known to have survived for the period between 1873 and 1844 in series ADM 196 (online at DocumentsOnline). However, many warrant officers went on to become commissioned officers, and so their records will be found among the records of officers' services.

Other Ranks

There are several series of records that might provide information:

- Records of service, 1842–1936 (ADM 159). These provide a marine's date and place of birth, trade, physical description, religion, date and place of enlistment and a full record of service with comments on conduct. These records are available through DocumentsOnline.
- Attestation forms, 1790–1925 (ADM 157). These are forms, compiled for each marine on enlistment. They give birthplace, previous occupation, physical description and often a record of service after attestation. To use them, however, you will need to know which division your man belonged to. A name index is slowly being added to TNA's online catalogue.
- Description books, c. 1755–1940 (ADM 158). On entry into service as a marine a description of every man was entered into the description books compiled from the information given on the attestation forms in ADM 157. However, the records will fill in the gaps where the attestation no longer exists and will give a reason and date of discharge.

Royal Marine commandos engage in a wartime training exercise 'somewhere in England'.
(Taylor Collection)

Registers of courts martial are in ADM 194. The records are for the Portsmouth and Plymouth divisions as well as for some marine units stationed overseas and run from 1812 to 1978. Provided you know roughly when the court martial took place, they can provide additional resources. Some earlier records are in ADM 13.

The Fleet Air Arm Museum also has some material for other ranks between about 1890 and 1920 (see Appendix 2). For details of those who enlisted after 1925, write to: Historical Records Office, Royal Marines, DPS(N)2, Building 1/152, Victory View, PP36, HMNB Portsmouth PO1 3PX.

Two World Wars
Some records of the Royal Marines for the First World War, including war diaries, are in ADM 137. Medals awarded to marines are in ADM 171/92 and online at Ancestry. A large party were interned in the Netherlands during the war after fleeing across the border after the Germans invaded Antwerp, which the marines had been defending. Interviews with a few of these men are in WO 161 (which are on DocumentsOnline) and some medical records are in MH 106.

Second World War diaries for RM units, including the Commandos, are in ADM 202 at Kew. There is some overlap with war diaries for combined operations in DEFE 2. Some files about the award of gallantry medals to Commandos are in ADM 1. Registers of marine deaths are in ADM 104/127-139. A list of Royal Marines known to have been held in German camps between 1939 and 1945 is to be found in ADM 201/111. The Royal Marines Museum also has an extensive collection of photographs, operational war diaries and other reports.

Further Reading

There are several excellent guides if you are researching marine ancestors, including Richard Brooks and Matthew Little's *Tracing Your Royal Marine Ancestors* (Pen & Sword, 2008). Another useful book is Ken Divall's *My Ancestor Was a Royal Marine* (Society of Genealogists, 2008). TNA have two In-depth Research Guides to Royal Marine officers and other ranks which can be downloaded from their website. In addition, the Royal Marines Museum's website also has many useful resources (see Appendix 5 for details).

Chapter 9

RESEARCHING SHIPS

At some stage you may want to find out more about the ships your ancestor served in and what his experiences were like on board. There are a lot of resources available that can help.

Resources

Reference Books and Service Histories

It is very easy to find out basic information about individual Royal Navy vessels. However, as many ships have carried the same name you need to roughly know when your ancestor was a member of the crew: there

HMS Cornwallis *bombards S Beach at Gallipoli, 1915.* (National Museum of the Royal Navy)

have been five *Ark Royals*, for example, beginning with the English flag ship at the Armada in 1588. The easiest thing is to type in the ship's name into Google or Bing. Normally, the first result will take you to an entry in Wikipedia which will provide brief details of the vessel. For the nineteenth and twentieth centuries a more informative alternative is to consult the database of RN ships after 1860 at www.battleships-cruisers.co.uk/royal.htm is, which has photographs that you can buy, and brief details about the ship as well as contributions from visitors to the site. You will need to scroll down the page to find what you want. The main site offers the same facility for most other navies of the world.

There are also a number of reference books, sometimes called service histories, providing brief histories of ships. The best known is J. J. Colledge's *Ships of the Royal Navy: A Complete Record of all Fighting Ships of the Royal Navy from the 15th Century to the Present* (4th edn, Casemate, 2010) which should be readily available in local reference libraries. However, it can be frustrating to use. Thousands of Royal Navy ships are listed in strict alphabetical order but with a minimum of detail. Where there have been a number of ships of the same name, the earliest is listed first. Facts against each ship's name include: type, displacement, length and breadth, number and size of guns, builder, date completed (or date purchased/acquired) and fate. There is no narrative, not even for those ships sunk in famous engagements.

There are also a number of more specialist books providing information on ships in considerably more detail. The specialist naval museums and archives are likely to have copies, but otherwise they can be hard to track down in public libraries. The guide to Royal Navy ships in the nineteenth century is David Lyon and Rif Winfield's *The Sail and Steam Navy List 1815–1889* (Chatham, 2003), which details every ship employed by the Royal Navy, whether purpose-built, taken from the enemy, purchased or hired. Organised by era, ship type and class, it is a useful resource for anyone with a query about British sailing and steam warships. It is extensively illustrated with a representative collection of original plans and collections at the National Maritime Museum. David Lyon also wrote *The Sailing Navy List: All the Ships of the Royal Navy – Built, Purchased and Captured, 1688–1855* (National Maritime Museum, 1993). Meanwhile, Rif Winfield also has a series of similar reference books to his name, including *British Warships in the Age of Sail 1603–1714: Design, Construction, Careers and Fates* (Seaforth, 2007), *British Warships in the Age of Sail 1715–1792: Design, Construction, Careers and Fates* (Seaforth, 2009) and *British Warships in the Age of Sail 1793–1817: Design, Construction, Careers and Fates* (Seaforth, 2008).

Probably of more immediate use are the brief histories of many of the ships that fought during the French Revolutionary and Napoleonic Wars at www.ageofnelson.org/MichaelPhillips/index.html. Often the names of the ship's commanders are given together with the final fate of the ship itself. Incidentally, the numbers in brackets after the ship's name refers to the number of guns she carried, i.e. HMS *Victory* (100). For the mid-Victorian Royal Navy many ships are listed and briefly described on the HMS *Surprise* website at www.pdavis.nl/MidVicShips.php?page=1. The site is not easy to navigate around: the trick is to click on the Background link at the top of each webpage.

For the twentieth century it may be worth looking out for Jane's *All the World's Fighting Ships* which has been publishing details of the ships under commission in the world's navies since 1898. These books are hard to come by and you can realistically only expect to find them in specialist naval libraries.

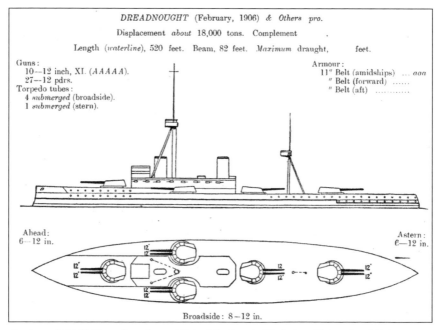

A plan of HMS Dreadought *published in* Jane's Fighting Ships *for 1906.* (Simon Fowler)

Fortunately, for ships that served during the Second World War look no further than the late Geoffrey Mason's 'Service Histories of Royal Navy Warships in World War 2'. It can be found towards the bottom of the homepage on the superb Naval History website: www.naval-history.net. Lt Cdr Mason provides an almost day-by-day account of each ship's activities together with a description of when she was built and her fate. Often there is an indication of any convoy escort duties that the ship undertook. The site also has much about ships of the First World War.

If you are at the National Maritime Museum, ask to see their 'Warship Histories', a microfiche compiled by museum staff, which lists alphabetically all British warships from c. 1650–1950. Entries include launch dates, size, number of men and guns and brief outlines of ship careers, with commanders. The NMM also has 'Twentieth Century Warship Histories', an unpublished typescript compiled by the Naval Historical Branch. It gives service summaries for Royal Navy vessels, with more detail on ships that served during the Second World War.

Websites

A search of Google for the ship you are interested in may turn up a website devoted to it, or, more likely, direct you to Wikipedia, where there are many pages about individual ships, although often enough entries are not always very detailed. There are also many websites devoted to the history of individual ships. Some are serious histories, particularly of the larger battlecruisers and battleships which took part in the great sea battles of the two world wars, but many are often overlaid with a heavy layer of nostalgia and really only appeal to former members of the ships' crews. Occasionally, there are sites devoted to the smaller and less well-known vessels such as HMS *Falcon*, one of the Royal Navy river gunboats that patrolled the Chinese waterways from the end of the nineteenth century until after the Second World War (www.hmsfalcon.com).

Admiralty Movement Books

These books at the National Maritime Museum (TNA does not seem to have any sets) cover the movements of Royal Navy ships (also vessels of the Royal Australian, Canadian and Indian navies) during the Second World War. They include vessels on government service down to trawlers, but not landing craft, hired vessels or troopships. The books are in two sequences: one for surviving vessels, another for those sunk. Both sets are in alphabetical order by name of ship. Vessels are distinguished by type as well as name, but there are some oddities; for example, many corvettes are listed simply as a 'patrol vessel'. Details of departures and arrivals are shown and may include convoy numbers, repairs and incidents such as crews rescued from torpedoed vessels. For trawlers used as minesweepers, movement details are restricted to transit between bases and there is little information on ship movements in the Pacific. It is possible that the Naval Museum Library in Portsmouth may also have sets.

However, TNA has various series of Navy lists for the wartime period and afterwards which give the location of ships, including the Pink List (so called from its cover) in ADM 187 which gives the location in port, though not position at sea, of all RN ships and Naval Air Squadrons in commission (these run between 1939 and 1976). Red Lists (ADM 208) detail all the minor war vessels in home waters under commands and include the vessels of allied countries. Green Lists (ADM 210) record landing ships, craft and barges in home waters and foreign stations under commands. Monthly Blue Lists in ADM 209 list ships under construction.

Navy List

The official *Navy List*, and its private rivals, shows Royal Navy ships, their commanders and officers, together with coastguard vessels, hired vessels and packet ships. Early nineteenth-century volumes also list French, Spanish and American ships taken during the Napoleonic Wars and British ships lost, captured or destroyed. A database containing details of Royal Naval ships listed in *Steel's Navy List* for 1794 is at www.nelsonsnavy.freesurf.fr.

Photographs and Paintings

Photographs of naval ships built between 1854 and 1954 are in series ADM 176, although larger and better collections are with the National Maritime Museum and, for the two world wars, the Imperial War Museum. The Royal Naval Museum Library has the Wright and Logan Collection of warship photographs, which consists of around 22,000 negatives, mostly on glass plates, of ships taken between 1924 and 1998.

The National Maritime Museum also has several collections of photographs of naval ships created by the Admiralty as well as by private

The commander and crew of HMS Iron Duke, *photographed on 28 November 1918.* (Viscount Jellicoe, *The Grand Fleet* (Cassell, 1920))

individuals. The Admiralty photographs are, in the main, the work of professional photographers and tend to concentrate on dockyard and warship-building activities as the majority of official wartime photographs showing life in the Navy were sent to the Imperial War Museum. Collections from other photographers, however, reflect the varied lives in the Royal Navy – training at naval training establishments as well as life on board ship both in peace and wartime.

Some officers and ratings, though usually the former, such as Cdr J. E. Manners, Earl Howe and Dr P. Ransome-Wallis took their cameras to war with them and so provide vital details about events, people and life in the Royal Navy at a time when photography was restricted by censorship. These and other photographers whose work is also at the NMM also documented foreign warships that they came into contact with on their travels around the world, both as enemies and allies.

The Royal Naval Museum also has several small collections of photographs relating to the building of naval ships, including negatives presented by the Admiralty and Portsmouth dockyard, showing the construction of HMS *Dreadnought* in 1906 and over 1,000 negatives of the building of HMS *Hampshire* in 1961. There is a NMM research guide which explains these records in more detail at http://tinyurl.com/23havg8.

There are also a number of websites that contain photographs of naval ships, such as the Steve Johnson Cyber Heritage pages at http://freepages.rootsweb.ancestry.com/~cyberheritage, which offer rather grainy images of many warships and submarines from the 1880s to the 1950s. Perhaps more useful is the Navy Photo site at www.navyphotos.co.uk, which contains a collection of naval photographs from the mid-nineteenth century until the millennium.

Another useful site is flickr (www.flickr.co.uk) which hosts tens of millions of photographs on a huge variety of topics (it is very easy to get side-tracked in your searches) posted by amateur and professional photographers as well as museums and attractions – Portsmouth Historic Dockyards has put up an interesting collection, for example. There are likely to be many more images for ships still in commission or recently decommissioned, than for historic vessels, but it is worth trying.

There has long been a fine maritime painting tradition which goes back to the seventeenth century. So if you are researching a ship before the introduction of photography in the mid-nineteenth century then you may find a panting of your ship generally shown in action or under sail. Paintings can of course be difficult to track down, but a good place is in the collections of the National Maritime Museum; its extensive collection of art and artefacts can be searched at www.nmm.ac.uk/collections/explore/index.cfm/category/art. For HMS *Bellerophon*, for example, the Museum has fifteen paintings about the ship or the men who commanded her.

Ships' Logs

Ships' logs go back centuries and record activities hour by hour. In general, they only note navigational and weather observations, although you may occasionally find descriptions of actions and other matters the captain thought to record. Until 1805, they began at midday each day, which was when a daily navigational reading was taken, but thereafter they commence at midnight.

These books are now proving an essential tool in the study of global warming because they record what the weather was like in parts of the world where there was no habitation. The Colonial Registers and Royal Navy Logbooks Project (CORRAL) has digitised a selection of logs as part of an assignment to understand how the climate changed during the eighteenth and nineteenth centuries. If you want to know more about this very interesting venture, visit http://badc.nerc.ac.uk/data/corral. A new project using ships' logs from the early twentieth century is at www.oldweather.org; they are looking for volunteers to help transcribe the records.

Logs begin in 1648 (at least these are the earliest at Kew). TNA has sets of captains', masters' and ships' logs up to 1981. However, there are some gaps for the Second World War where, apart for the early months of the war, logs do not survive for ships smaller than cruisers (such as destroyers and minesweepers). In addition, logs were not kept by ships undergoing major refit, which may account for some gaps in sequence. They are arranged in several series (which may contain subtly different information) and then by ship and date:

- ADM 50 – admirals' journals (1702–1916).
- ADM 51 – captains' logs (1669–1852). These were maintained by the captain of each ship in commission, and cover details of the employment and position of the ship and ship's company, details of weather encountered and provide a full picture of the daily routine of a naval vessel under sail. Some occasionally provide a list of the crew.
- ADM 52 – masters' logs (1672–1840). These were maintained by the Sailing Master as a record of the ship's course, position, weather encountered, employment of the hands and record of punishments carried out. They also recorded any discrepancies found when opening casks of food or drink (not an uncommon occurrence) to make subsequent claims against suppliers. Other masters' logs are in ADM 54 (1808–71).
- ADM 53 – ships' logs (1799–1985). These were maintained by the Officer of the Watch of every ship in commission and provide a daily record of the ships' movements and position, listing all wheel and telegraph orders, weather encountered and other events, such as the employment of the ship's company. Also recorded are any deaths on board, disciplinary action (that is the reading of punishment warrants), loss or damage to stores and any other items of interest, such as visits by dignitaries or foreign officers.
- ADM 55 – logs from ships engaged in exploration, both logs (navigational records) and journals (narrative accounts) of naval officers of ships engaged in exploration and surveying. Most were kept by

Hours	Knots	Tenths	Courses	Lee way in points	Winds	Force	Weather	Barometer or Sympiesometer	Thermometer	Remarks	Initials of Officer of the Watch
1	7	·			*Nly*	4	b c				
2	6	5									
3	5	·									
4	5	4			*Nly*	4	b c				
5	6	·									
6	6	2									
7	6	"									
8	5	·			*Nly*	4	b c				
9	5	5									
10	5	5									
11	5	1									
12	5	1			*Nly*	4	b c	30/18	66		

Course	Distance	Latitude by		Longitude by			Bearing and Distance at Noon	
		D. R.	Obs.	D. R.	Chron.	Lunars		
	154	30.17 a	30.16 a	10.30 E	10.50 E			

1	5	2			*South*	3	b cv.				
2	5	·									
3	5	"									
4	5	·									
5	6	·									
6	6	2									
7	7	"			*South*	3	b cm.				
8	5	"									
9	6	·									
10	5	·									
11	3	4									
12	3	2									

Note.—The Knots are to consist of 10 instead of 8 divisions.

The Columns for the force of the Wind and for the Weather are to be filled in conformity with the Scheme in the First Page of this Book.

See Admiralty Instructions, page 173, Art. 1st, and 213, Art. 19.

A page from the log of HMS Apollo *for March 1851. Originally a fifth-rate frigate with thirty-eight guns, by the time of this entry she had long been a troopship. (TNA ADM 53/3598)* naval captains, masters, lieutenants and masters mates. There are a few others, kept by boatswains or assistant surgeons. Many famous officers appear here: James Cook, William Bligh and Matthew Flinders, among them.

In addition, some very early logs are in ADM 7 and logs for submarines are in ADM 173.

With some exceptions you will need to visit to Kew to read these records. However, CORRAL (http://badc.nerc.ac.uk/data/corral) has digitised all of the logs in ADM 55 (also in DocumentsOnline, but here there is a charge of £2 to download these records) and a selection of logs in ADM 53. However, they have not been indexed or transcribed so you will have to go through the logs page by page to find what you are looking for.

In addition, the National Maritime Museum has lieutenants' logs from 1673–1809, although they are not complete. The Museum's Manuscripts Section has a detailed index, but it is not online. Like the logs at TNA, they record weather, navigation and ship routines, as well as incidents occurring during a ship's commission, such as loss or damage to stores and disciplinary action.

Shipwrecks and Naval Disasters

Even today it is all too easy for ships to be lost at sea or run aground, collide with other ships and be involved in all manner of accidents. As might be expected, the weather is the single biggest cause of disaster and is probably the reason behind the majority of unexplained disappearances of ships: in most cases they almost certainly succumbed to storms. There are innumerable examples of ships being lost in this way. HMS *Resolution* was one of thirteen ships that the Royal Navy lost in the Great Storm of 1703 in south-east England. HMS *Centaur* foundered in a hurricane in 1782, taking 400 crew to their deaths. Her captain, John Inglefield, with a handful of men, managed to pilot the ship's pinnace to the Azores without any navigational aids and only two quarts of drinking water – a journey of sixteen days in an open boat.

Human error is another factor, particularly where there is a navigational miscalculation. Such mistakes can be embarrassing – for example, HMS *Arethusa* was lost in 1779 when her captain mistook shore lights for an enemy vessel at night and ran his ship onto rocks off the coast of France. In February 1852, the ironclad troopship

The loss of the Royal George *off Spithead in August 1782 saw the deaths of many hundreds of sailors, as well as their families and other local people who had come aboard to say their farewells before the ship sailed.* (Henry J. Sparks, *The Story of Portsmouth* (Portsmouth, 1921))

HMS *Birkenhead* was lost off the coast of South Africa with the loss of nearly 450 of the ship's crew and soldiers having been dashed on rocks in calm weather. The women and children on board were safely boarded into the ship's few lifeboats and made it to shore, while the soldiers on board impassively awaited their fate. This led to what has become known as the 'Birkenhead Drill' –women and children should be rescued first.

For even the most minor incident there should be a court of enquiry held to investigate circumstances, apportion blame if applicable, but more importantly make recommendations to prevent any repetition of the event. Courts martial were always held in the case of the loss of a ship. Records of these enquiries are at TNA, although they may not always be easy to find. Those for the Second World War may be in series WO 199, for the First World War in WO 137 or for the first half of the twentieth century in ADM 178 (from 1892–1951), or in ADM 1 and ADM 116. You are more likely to find enquiries before the 1840s in ADM 1 and thereafter in ADM 116, but there is some overlap between the series and even wartime enquiries may be found here as well. For the more important or interesting enquiries there may also be press coverage.

There are a number of reference books devoted to ships lost at sea, including W. P. Gosset's *The Lost Ships of the Royal Navy 1793–1900*

(Mansell, 1986), which includes details of any subsequent courts martial (see also Paul Benyon's list of ships at http://tinyurl.com/67rb247); David Hepper's *War Ship Losses during the Age of Sail 1650–1859* (Chatham, 1994); David Hepper's *British Warship Losses in the Ironclad Era: 1860–1919* (Chatham, 2006); Charles Hocking's *Dictionary of Disasters at Sea During the Age of Steam Including Sailing Ships and Ships of War Lost in Action, 1824–1962* (2 vols, Lloyds Register of Shipping, 1969); and for the Second World War, John M. Young's *Britain's Sea War: A Diary of Ship Losses, 1939–1945* (Patrick Stephens, 1989). Extracts from news reports in *The Times* of the few naval vessels lost during the 1860s can be found at www.pdavis.nl/Background.htm.

Ephemera

Badges

After the First World War ships increasingly acquired officially approved badges which were displayed in prominent places on board. The first one officially sanctioned was for HMS *Tower* in 1917. They can be seen as the successors to the figureheads which were once proudly carried by men-of-war. Many designs are very attractive and are often based on heraldic themes. There are several websites that display collections of ships' badges, including www.ships-badges.co.uk, www.admirals.org.uk/forkids/badges/index.php and www.militaryfigures.co.uk. Facsimile badges are readily available for sale from these sites. Those for ships of the Second World War period are described in Geoffrey Mason's 'Service Histories' (see p. 141).

Commissioning Books

During the twentieth century the habit grew up of producing special commemorative books, known as commissioning books, to record voyages with photographs and text. They were paid for from ships' welfare funds. This practice was, however, not universal and not every ship did this. Although they are full of in-jokes and now rather dated humour, they can be a fascinating insight into life on board. There is no national collection or seemingly a systematic attempt to collect them, which is a pity, but small collections may be found at naval museums. Plymouth library also has a collection. The equivalent for Fleet Air Arm squadrons is line books, of which the FAA Museum has extensive holdings.

Some mainly post-war examples are online at www.axfordsabode. org.uk/rnships.htm. Examples of photograph albums compiled during a world tour undertaken by the First Light Cruiser Squadron in 1923 and 1924 are at www.navyphotos.co.uk/index26%20world%20cruise.htm and http://sites.google.com/site/worldcruise19231924. A few books are for sale at www.rjerrard.co.uk/royalnavy/cbooks/cbooks.html. Others may be on sale through eBay and other sites.

Old and new: HMS Victory *with HMS* Dauntless *in the background, Portsmouth dockyard, October 2010.* (Simon Fowler)

Chapter 10

HM DOCKYARDS

For decades in the eighteenth and nineteenth centuries the Admiralty (the Navy Board before 1832) was the largest employer in Britain, providing jobs for thousands of men at its dockyards around southern England. Indeed, the Navy Board may well have run the largest industrial concern in the world at the time and as a result played a major role in Britain's industrialisation, although it is one that is still little understood. The block mills at Portsmouth dockyard, for example, formed the first steam-powered factory, using what became known as mass-production techniques making ships' blocks, when it opened in 1803.

There were a dozen or so naval dockyards across the British Isles and in a number of places in the Empire as well, such as Malta and Gibraltar. These dockyards built many of the Navy's ships, repaired and maintained them and prepared them for service at sea.

Two craftsmen at Portsmouth just after the First World War. (National Museum of the Royal Navy)

There were also a number of private merchant yards, which built ships either to the Admiralty's design (supervised by a foreman from a naval dockyard), to their own design hoping to sell it to the Admiralty or as a merchant ship that the Navy bought and converted. Occasionally, they would use yards outside the British Isles, for example, the second-rate man-of-war HMS Ganges was built in Bombay by the master shipbuilder Jamsetjee Bomanjee Wadia between 1819 and 1821. There is a fine model of the ship at the National Maritime Museum.

In the mid-eighteenth century it took about six months to build a sloop, two to three years for a two-decker and several years for a First Rate. After the launch ceremony, the fitting out, or supplying of masts, rigging, sails, guns, boats, stores and so on, could take several months more. But this timetable might be delayed by financial constraints or the conclusion of a war. The *Victory*, for example, was laid down in Chatham dockyard in October 1759 but construction was stopped a few months later. It only restarted in 1763 and she was finally launched in May 1765.

The oldest and most important dockyard has always been at Portsmouth, where a naval dry dock was built as early as 1496 to allow warships to be drawn out of the water so that their hulls might be repaired and cleaned. It was important both for the construction of warships and the provision of repair and maintenance facilities. In addition, its harbour was used for the laying-up of warships in time of peace (as is still the case today), while the Spithead anchorage served as a rendezvous point for convoys in wartime. It has also been a major employer, with nearly 3,000 men working there in 1776 (quite possibly the largest number of men employed by a single employer at a single location at the time). At its peak in 1918 it employed 25,000 craftsmen and labourers.

Originally established in the 1690s, by the late-eighteenth century, Plymouth had become the second largest dockyard and was also involved in the construction of new warships. In addition, it helped maintain ships of the Channel Fleet, serving as a base for cruising squadrons of the Atlantic, whether blockading France at the end of the eighteenth century or on convoy duty during two world wars.

Because it was so close to the Admiralty and Navy Board in London, Deptford was particularly important. It was, for example, the yard most frequently chosen for any new experimental work, with members of the Navy Board easily able to visit the yard in order to monitor progress. The yard was also responsible for supplying naval equipment to other Royal dockyards, both at home and abroad, until it closed in 1869.

The introduction of steam ships led to a total revolution in the dockyards with new techniques and trades and giant new steam yards, where the new vessels were built and serviced. The first was at Woolwich, which opened in 1831. Other steam yards were built at Devonport (as the yard at Plymouth was re-named in 1843) and Portsmouth. During the 1860s, a massive 380-acre extension was constructed at Chatham. It was geared to the needs of steam-powered iron battleships, and consisted of numerous workshops and factory buildings located around three enclosed basins and four dry docks. If you want to know more, the challenges of technological change in the nineteenth century Navy is explored by Phil Russell in an interesting website, although it has not been updated for a while, at www. btinternet.com / ~philipr / content.htm.

Rosyth dockyard in Fife is by far the most recent naval dockyard with construction work beginning in 1909. It was designed to provide fleet maintenance facilities in the event of war with Germany when it was completed in 1916. Some early records of the yard and photographs are

The construction of HMS Dreadnought *in Portsmouth dockyard, October 1905.*
(National Museum of the Royal Navy)

now with the National Archives of Scotland. www.nas.gov.uk/about/0708013.asp.

The First World War saw the dockyards mainly engaged in repair and refit work, although a considerable number of new ships were launched from the slipways of Portsmouth, Pembroke, Chatham (mainly submarines) and Devonport. However, post-war economies saw the temporary closure of both Rosyth and Pembroke.

The approach of war in 1939 saw the re-establishment of Pembroke and Rosyth, together with an expansion of the workforce in all the other yards. Over the next 5 years the Royal dockyards laid down over 30 new ships and carried out more than 97,000 refits. However, Pembroke and Sheerness were permanently closed in 1947 and 1960 respectively. Chatham closed in 1984. Now naval repairs are carried out at Portsmouth, Plymouth and Rosyth with private contractors, such as Vickers at Barrow-in-Furness, building what new ships are still being commissioned.

If you are interested, the Naval Dockyards Society encourages research into the history of the dockyards and campaigns for their preservation. Find out more at http://navaldockyards.moonfruit.com. Brief histories and old photographs of many of HM dockyards in Britain and across the Empire can be found at www.battleships-cruisers.co.uk/devonport_dockyard.htm.

The dockyards at Chatham and Portsmouth are now major tourist attractions. If you visit the Historic Dockyards in Portsmouth there is a fascinating exhibition on the lives and occupations of the dockyard workers, and a superb website with lots about the dockyards' history at www.portsmouthdockyard.org.uk. Details about visiting the Chatham and Portsmouth docks are given in Appendix 5.

There's lots about Plymouth and its dockyard at Steve Johnson's Cyber Heritage pages at www.cyber-heritage.co.uk, although the website is, to put it mildly, eccentrically arranged. And a 1796 guide to Plymouth dockyard for tourists is available on Google Books; read it at http://tinyurl.com/62e9t4x.

The Records

More about researching ancestors who worked in the naval dockyards can be found in the TNA In-depth Research Guide *Royal Naval Dockyards*, which can be downloaded from TNA's website.

It can be helpful to understand how the dockyards were run in order to see how your ancestor fitted into a large and at times confusing

Portsmouth dockyard looking west, early twentieth century. (National Museum of the Royal Navy)

organisation. Until its abolition in 1832, dockyards and naval establishments were the responsibility of the Navy Board, a body technically subordinate to the Admiralty, but in practice an independent entity. The Navy Board had two subsidiary boards, the Victualling, and Sick and Hurt, with their members also appointed by the Admiralty Board. The Victualling Board appointed pursers and supplied the Navy with food, drink and clothes, using its own bakeries, breweries and slaughterhouses, and ran victualling yards within or adjacent to the dockyards. The Sick and Hurt Board examined surgeons, provided their supplies and ran the hospitals, and looked after and exchanged prisoners of war (see Chapter 7).

However, the gun-wharves belonged to the Ordnance Board, an entirely independent body responsible only to the Master-General of Ordnance. When the Ordnance Board was abolished in 1855, control of naval ordnance passed to the War Office. Responsibility for its own gunnery supplies was assumed by the Admiralty as late as 1909.

Dockyards were originally run by naval officers who were civilian employees of the Navy Board, not sea officers and who were sometimes referred to as 'yard officers'. The senior official of each yard was the Commissioner, appointed by, and nominally a member of, the Navy

Board. Under him were the Clerk of the Cheque and the Storekeeper, who with their clerks were responsible for the financial and administrative business of the yard; the Master Shipwright, who with his colleagues the Master Sailmaker, Anchorsmith, Rigger, Boatbuilder, etc., was in charge of the building and repair work of the yard; the Master Attendants and the Boatswain, who supervised the yard craft, the ships afloat and 'in Ordinary', that is in reserve; and finally the Master Ropemaker who ran the ropeyard.

These senior officers, together with the clerks and foremen known as Inferior Officers, were salaried, as were the established artificers and labourers of the yard; unestablished employees were borne on the Extraordinary vote. Although yard officers were naval and not sea officers, there was movement between the two services. The Commissioners and Masters Attendant were usually retired sea officers; dockyard shipwrights, having served their apprenticeship, often became carpenters in the Navy, and might return to be Master Shipwrights, and in the same way the other Master Tradesmen and the Boatswain were normally recruited from the Sea Service. The career of many skilled men can often be traced though records relating to the Navy as well as dockyards.

The senior officers of a victualling yard, responsible for fitting out ships prior to sailing, were the Agent Victualler (larger establishments only), the Storekeeper or Naval Officer and the Clerk of the Cheque. In addition, there might also have been the Transport Agents, Agents for Prisoners and Hospital Agents who represented the Transport Board and the Sick and Hurt Board. Each of these had their own clerks and labourers.

After the abolition of the Navy Board in 1832, all yards and establishments in each port, excepting the gun-wharves, were amalgamated under a single authority, though the victualling yards continued in practice to remain distinct. The senior officer of each yard was now the Superintendent, generally an admiral or captain-superintendent, according to the size of the yard. He was a serving sea officer and was often also the Port Admiral, that is the local flag officer.

The introduction of steam ships led to the building of 'steam factories' attached to the major yards, with an Inspector of Steam Machinery and a Captain of the Steam Reserve joining the Admiral Superintendent's subordinates. Later, the steam factories were integrated into the yards, and a Chief Constructor took the place of the Inspector of Steam Machinery and the Master Shipwright. Though many titles have since changed, the yards continue to be run by a mixed body of civilians and sea officers under the authority of the Admiral Superintendent.

The main series of records for the larger yards before 1832 (and in some cases later) is the Yard Pay Books (ADM 42) and those for minor yards and establishments are the Ships' Pay Books, Ticket Office (ADM 32) and the Ships' Musters (ADM 36 and ADM 37), all of which are arranged by yard. In addition, there are some miscellaneous records arranged by trade in ADM 6, ADM 30, ADM 106 and ADM 107.

For victualling yards, try the Victualling Departments Registers (ADM 113) and Victualling Yards: Portsmouth and Gosport (ADM 224). Salaries between 1805 and 1822 are recorded in ADM 7/869-871. Some records of men who were employed by the Board of Ordnance in dockyards are in WO 54.

More about the running of dockyards before 1832 can be found in the detailed records of the Navy Board in ADM 106 and ADM 354. A project is taking place to catalogue properly the in-letters in ADM 106 for much of the eighteenth century, which when complete will make an important series of records much easier to use.

After 1832, the main series of records are in Additional Pension Books (ADM 23) and Naval Establishment: Salaried Officers Civil Pensions (PMG 24), and roughly go up to the early 1920s. Incidentally, if your ancestor was working in the yards in the mid-nineteenth century it is still worth looking at the Yard Pay Books in ADM 42. Information about Naval Store and Ordnance Officers (1857–1914) is in ADM 7/917 and about Civil Appointments between 1860 and 1870 is in ADM 7/920. There are also pension registers in ADM 23 from 1830–1926, and PMG 25 from 1836–1928.

Some service records for dockyard personnel between 1892 and 1939 are with the Directorate of Personnel Support (Navy), Navy Search, TNT Archive Services, Tetron Point, William Nadin Way, Swadlincote DE11 0BB. Promotions of skilled men may be recorded in the *London Gazette* between about 1870 and 1920 (see Chapter 2 for more details). Many dockyard workers received medals (often the Imperial Service Medal, a precursor of the OBE) which again were recorded in the *Gazette*.

The dockyards were dangerous places to work. Dockyard workers could be treated at naval hospitals for their injuries (see Chapter 7) and deductions were taken from their wages to pay for it. Some of the men whose bodies now lie in the burial ground at Haslar may well have fallen from scaffolding or from ships to the bottom of the dry docks. Such injuries to the dockyard workforce were common. A certificate for the apprentice William Powell, a carpenter, found in the Navy Board in-letters, dated June 1769 reads:

> Powell received a partial Dislocation of the upper Vertebra of the Loins, by a Piece of thick stuff falling upon him as he was assisting to put it into the Kiln; which compressed the Spinal Marrow, and occasioned an immediate Palsey of the lower Limbs, attended by a violent suppression of urine, and an Ulcer of the Bladder, which not only confined him to his Bed, but greatly endangered his Life, and thereby occasioned an inevitable loss of time, till the 21st May following. (TNA, ADM 106/1183/193)

Chatham dockyard in its mid-eighteenth-century heyday. (Simon Fowler)

NAVAL RATINGS

The Royal Navy has always been made up of a very large number of different ratings. The list below shows the various ranks and titles in existence in 1853.

Chief Petty Officer

Master at Arms
Chief Gunner's Mate
Chief Boatswain's Mate
Chief Captain of the Forecastle
Admiral's Coxswain
Chief Stoker

Chief Quartermaster
Chief Yeoman of the Signals
Chief Carpenter's Mate
Seaman's Schoolmaster
Ship's Cook
Chief Bandmaster

Petty Officers 1st Class

Ship's Corporal
Gunner's Mate
Boatswain's Mate
Captain's Coxswain
Captain of the Forecastle
Quartermaster
Coxswain of the Launch
Captain of the Foretop
Captain of the Maintop
Captain of the Afterguard

Captain of the Hold
Sailmaker
Ropemaker
Carpenter's Mate
Caulker
Blacksmith
Leading Stoker
Painter 1st Class
Plumber
Shipwright

Petty Officer 2nd Class

Coxswain of the Barge
Coxswain of the Pinnace
Captain of the Mast
Painter 2nd Class

2nd Captain of the Forecastle
Sailmaker's Mate
Coxswain of the Cutter
Cooper

Armourer

Caulker's Mate

2nd Captain of the Foretop

2nd Captain of the Maintop

2nd Captain of the Afterguard

Yeoman of the Signals

Captain of the Mizentop

Painter

Musician

Plumber's Mate

Head Krooman

Other Ratings

Leading Seaman

Yeoman of the Storeroom

Yeoman of the Tiers

2nd Captain of the Hold

Sick Berth Attendant

Sailmaker's Crew

Blacksmith's Mate

Armourer's Crew

Stoker and Coal Trimmer

Carpenter's Crew

Cooper's Crew

Able Seaman

Bandsman

Butcher

Tailor

Plumber's Crew

2nd Head Krooman

Captain's Steward

Ward or Gunroom Steward

Ward or Gunroom Cook

Subordinate Officer's Steward

Subordinate Officer's Cook

Ship's Steward's Assistant

Ordinary Seaman

Cook's Mate

Barber

Second Class Ordinary Seaman

Krooman

Boy First Class

Boy Second Class

There were a number of other ratings that had been abolished only a few years before:

Trumpeter

Gunsmith

Midshipman Ordinary

Coxswain's Mate

Swabber

Ordinary Trumpeter

Shifter

Gunner's Tailor

Yeoman of Powder Room

Yeoman of Sheets

Quartermaster's Mate

Bugler

Cooper's Mate

Gunner's Yeoman

Ship's Tailor

Landsman

Taken from W. E. May, W. Y. Carman and John Tanner, *Badges and Insignia of the British Armed Services* (Adam and Charles Black, 1974), pp. 116–17.

Appendix 2

ROYAL NAVY AND ROYAL MARINES SERVICE DOCUMENTS AT THE FLEET AIR ARM MUSEUM

This appendix is based on a minute prepared for the Fleet Air Arm Museum (FAAM) in July 2009, which is available at www.fleetairarm.com/en-GB/royal_navy_royal_marines_services_documents.aspx.

The majority of records are non-commissioned personnel who enlisted in the Royal Navy and Royal Marines before about 1925. The earliest records date from the late 1850s. Included are the papers of most of the men who were enlisted for short service 'hostilities only' during the First World War.

The following are the main categories of these documents now held by the Museum's Centre for Naval Aviation Records and Research (see Appendix 5 for contact details).

Royal Navy

Engagement ledgers for Continuous Service (CS), Non-Continuous Service (NCS) and Special Service (SS) ratings. They cover most branches, including Seamen, Stokers, Artificers, Artisans, Ship's Police, Sick Berth Attendants. The period covered by these papers is 1888–1923, but this varies by branch.

Among the more unusual ledgers held are: those for men of many branches who transferred to the post-First World War Mine Clearance Service (MCS) as well as men who entered the MCS from shore; men who enlisted in First World War as WT operators, many from the Marconi Company; men who served in, or were transferred to, the navies of Canada and Australia; and for men who were transferred to the RAF on its formation but whose transfers were later annulled.

The Museum also holds papers (promotion and periodic reports) on nearly 350 Gunners RN covering a period from 1870 through to the Second World War.

Royal Naval Reserve (RNR)

Original record cards for RNR officers: Executive (X); Engineers (E); Cadets (from Pangbourne College only); Warrant Officer Telegraphists. Original record cards (and index ledgers) for most RNR rating categories (1908–55, but some as late as 1966). TNA has copies in BT 377.

The FAAM also has index cards for RNR ratings who served in the Second World War. Many men appear in both ledger and card indexes.

Royal Naval Volunteer Reserve (RNVR)

Engagement ledgers for the following categories:

- RNVR Divisions (Bristol, Clyde, London, Mersey, Sussex, Tyneside and Wales), pre-First World War Divisional Companies and wartime entry 'Z' ratings.
- Volunteer entrants in 1914 and 1915 to Crystal Palace/Royal Naval Division (RND) (KP, KW and KX ratings); civilian entrants to the RND (ZW and ZX ratings); Army (conscripted) entrants to RND (R ratings); civilian entrants at Crystal Palace (PZ and ZP ratings); Anti-aircraft Corps (AA ratings); Motor Boat Section (MB ratings); Birmingham Electrical Volunteers (E ratings).

Royal Naval Air Service (RNAS)

RNAS ratings: engagement ledgers for some 6,500 ratings who did not transfer to the RAF in April 1918 or who were commissioned.

RNAS officers and ratings: a comprehensive database of RNAS personnel has been compiled at the FAAM, drawing on numerous published and unpublished sources. The database is complemented by files on individuals where this is warranted by the amount of data available. Files on personnel 'attached to RNAS' are also included.

Men, of various branches including RNAS, who were transferred to the RAF on its formation but whose transfers were later annulled.

Royal Marines

These papers (sometimes referred to as 'Attestation Packs') may contain a very extensive record of a man's service from attestation to discharge, with a wealth of data in between amounting to a snapshot of military life and contemporary society in the early decades of the twentieth century. Records of individual marines can run as late as 1958, although most are before 1926. The papers are very comprehensive for men who served in or were recalled for the Second World War. Those records of service in Second World War Defensively Equipped Merchant Ships (DEMS) are probably unique.

There are also some admission and discharge papers for members of the RM Light Infantry and RM Artillery, which complement records at TNA in series ADM 157.

The Royal Marines Museum has a leaflet that describes these records in more detail at http://tinyurl.com/37rmuzc.

Other Branches

Royal Naval Division (Divisional Engineers, Divisional Train, RM Medical Unit and Ordnance Company) Deal Short Service – Register Numbers Deal/1(S) to Deal/5900(S). Note: in addition to service papers, there are also Royal Naval Division (RND) record cards for most of these men.

Royal Naval School of Music Continuous (Long) Service – Register Numbers RMB/1 to RMB/3100.

Royal Marines Labour Corps (RMLC) (New) Short Service – Register Numbers Deal/1N to Deal/1400N. This corps served in France during 1919: most records are at TNA in ADM 157.

Naval Papers

RN and RNVR ratings' papers are bound in volumes (engagement ledgers) in service number order and generally contain original attestation or enlistment papers. However, some individual records can be more extensive. In particular, the RNVR records of ratings who served with the RND usually contain original Active Service Casualty Forms (Army Form B.103), the contents of which were typed onto the RND record cards, and there may be other administrative correspondence.

Royal Naval Division Record Cards

The originals of the RND record cards which are in ADM 339 (and online) are now at the FAAM. However, the version at TNA contains numerous filing errors and some cards have not been copied correctly. Very few RMLI cards are in the main RND card archive but some are held with an individual's papers. For the RM Deal Short Service men of the Divisional Engineers, Divisional Train, RM Medical Unit and Ordnance Company of the RND a separate RND record card archive has been formed. TNA does not have copies of these cards.

Naval Records in Manuscript Ledgers

FAAM has an extensive series of nearly one-hundred First World War pay and appointing ledgers for officers of the RNVR, RNR and RNAS. These can offer useful information on pay and movements (including tax bills and probate) to complement records at Kew.

Other ledger records include:

- Crew books for Royal Fleet Auxiliary (RFA) and Mercantile Fleet Auxiliary (MFA), 1915–20 approximately. These contain alphabetical indexes of ships, crew lists (entries and discharges), rates of pay, next of kin, etc.
- RNVR Temporary Officers, Military Branch, 1917–19 approximately and Temporary Assistant Paymasters RNVR, 1914–19 approximately.
- Record of RNVR officers entered before First World War.
- Register of Officers of RNVR London Division, post-First World War.
- RNVR Chaplains' Record of Service.
- Personnel reports on gunners and warrant officers, 1911–31.
- Indexes of First World War ships, depots and bases including trawlers and defensively armed merchant ships (DAMS), 1912–19 approximately.
- RNR ratings indexes.
- RNAS indexes, including First World War death indexes.

Current Status

Many of the records received from the MoD were in poor condition, some having been neglected and badly stored for decades in damp conditions. A decade-long programme of conservation and indexing has been completed for all RM records. This work has ensured that the many hundreds of thousands of papers (the RMLI Continuous Service papers alone cover some 63,000 service numbers) are properly cared for and indexed.

The papers described above are available to researchers by prior arrangement. Researchers must check in advance that the service/ register number sought is in the series held by the FAAM and is not among those held, for example, by TNA.

The Museum also has microfilm copies of many of the most important record series at TNA for researching naval ancestors.

Appendix 3

MERCHANT SEAFARERS

Many ratings in particular made voyages in merchant ships, particularly before 1853, or merchant seamen volunteered for service in the Royal Navy Reserve during the two world wars (see Chapter 6). Here is a brief guide, although researching merchant seamen in particular is not always easy.

Most records are at TNA, although if you are interested in the ships your ancestor sailed on the National Maritime Museum is probably the best place to start. It helps if you know which ships he served on and whether he was an officer or just an ordinary crew member (and what his specialism was: engineer, radio operator and so on). A number of series of records have been digitised and are online through DocumentsOnline, while others are due to appear on Findmypast.

The earliest records date from 1747, when ships' musters and log books first had to be kept and they include lists of crew members. Unfortunately, few early books survive – those that do are in series BT 98. Seamen registered with the Board of Trade between 1835 and 1857 and these records are in various series between BT 112 and BT 120. Indexes of seamen and the ships they served on for the nineteenth century are being prepared by the Crew List Transcription Project at www.crewlist.org.uk/crewlist.html, and one or two family history societies – such as the Cornish – have also produced indexes for men from their county. Details of 23,000 Welsh mariners between 1800 and 1945 can be found at www.welshmariners.org.uk.

Details of seamen between 1858 and 1912 are found in the agreements and crew lists for individual ships. TNA has a 10 per cent sample. However, the largest collection of these records is with the Maritime History Archive, Memorial University of Newfoundland, St John's, NL A1B 3Y1, Canada; www.mun.ca/mha. There are also numerous other short-lived series of records between 1835 and 1913 at TNA, which may also provide information.

Service records for those who served in the Merchant Navy during the First World War are virtually non-existent. Record cards from the Central

Papers and a medal belonging to my grandfather Paul Belcher Fowler who served in the Merchant Navy in the years before and during the First World War. (Simon Fowler)

Index Register, covering the period 1913–20, were destroyed some time ago. All that survives are the cards from a special index for 1918–21. Each card usually gives name, place and date of birth, a short description and a photograph of the man. However, you can glean basic information from the Medal Index Cards recording the award of war medals, which are available on DocumentsOnline and in BT 351.

The Central Index Register of Seamen between 1921 and 1941 in BT 348 includes details of all categories of people (men and women) employed at sea, not just ordinary seamen, but also mates, engineers, trimmers, stewards, cooks, etc. The surviving cards are unusual in that they usually include a photograph of the individual together with a date and place of birth, rating, a brief physical description and a list of ships served on. A name index is also available through TNA's online catalogue. If you are interested, the originals are at Southampton City Archives (http://tinyurl.com/yloldc7). A database of Irish mariners of the early 1920s based on the Index is at www.irishmariners.ie. An excellent blog about one man's experiences in the Merchant Navy at this time is at http://monkbarns.wordpress.com.

The more recent Central Register of Seamen from 1942–72 comprises docket books and seamen's pouches in series BT 373 and BT 382. The books contain an entry for each seafarer and are arranged alphabetically under several headings. The pouches contain records relating to an individual seaman. An index is also available through TNA's online catalogue. DocumentsOnline also has details of campaign medals issued to merchant seamen for service during the Second World War, as well as movement cards for individual ships. These indicate the voyages a ship took.

Lloyd's Captains' Registers can be used for information on masters and mates. They are kept at the Guildhall Library in the City of London, although partial indexes are online at www.history.ac.uk/gh/capintro.htm.

The *Registers* are also the main source for information on foreign-going masters and mates between 1851 and 1947. The registers themselves are kept at Guildhall Library in London, with an incomplete set of microfilm copies at Kew.

Further Reading

More details about researching merchant seamen can be found at www.mariners-l.co.uk/UKMasters.html. Indeed, the whole site is full of valuable information about researching seamen of all ranks. Also of interest is Len Barnett's guide at www.barnettmaritime.co.uk/main.htm. In addition, TNA produces a series of readers' signposts and research guides that explain these records in more detail.

There are also several excellent publications, including Chris and Michael Watts's *My Ancestor was a Merchant Seaman* (Society of Genealogists, 2004) and Kelvin Smith et al.'s *Records of Merchant Seamen and Shipping* (Public Record Office, 1998).

Appendix 4

JACKSPEAK

One of the problems in researching the Royal Navy is the language. The English used on board ship, in dockyards and at the Admiralty – known colloquially as Jackspeak – is very different to that we landlubbers use. Many terms date back centuries and have been adapted as new technologies have been introduced. As a result, it can sometimes be difficult to understand what is meant, particularly if you are reading any naval social history or the memoirs for old sailors. Who, or what, for example was the 'Captain of the Heads'. In fact, he was the unfortunate man who was assigned to clean the toilets and no officer at all.

The Royal Navy has webpages devoted to naval slang (and explanations of naval service in general) at www.royalnavy.mod.uk/training-and-people/rn-life/navy-slang/index.htm A number of expressions current in the eighteenth-century Navy and later are explained at www.hmsrichmond.org/avast/customs.htm. Another selection of terms is given at www.navy-net.co.uk/wiki2/index.php/Category:Jackspeak. There are also several books that can help. The best guide (and certainly the most amusing) is probably Rick Jolly's *Jackspeak* (Maritime Books, 2000), although Martin Robson's *Not Enough Room to Swing a Cat: Naval Slang and Its Everyday Usage* (Conway Maritime, 2008) is also useful. A more serious approach is taken by John Hard in *Royal Navy Language* (Book Guild, 1991). Very dated, as it was first published in 1867, is Vice Admiral W. H. Smyth's *The Sailor's Wordbook* (Conway, 1981 and now in paperback).

Appendix 5

USEFUL ADDRESSES

Archives

British Library, 96 Euston Road, London NW1 2DB; tel: 020 7412 7000; www.bl.uk.

British Library Newspapers, Colindale Avenue, London NW9 5HE; tel: 020 7412 7353: www.bl.uk. The Library will be closed during 2012 and the resources removed to the out-station at Boston Spa near Leeds.

Commonwealth War Graves Commission, 2 Marlow Road, Maidenhead SL6 7DX; tel: 016 2850 7200; www.cwgc.org.

The National Archives, Ruskin Avenue, Kew, Richmond TW9 4DU; tel: 020 8876 3444; www.nationalarchives.gov.uk.

Society of Genealogists, 14 Charterhouse Buildings, Goswell Road, London EC1M 7BA; tel: 020 7251 8799; www.sog.org.uk.

Military Museums and Archives

These museums are not only major visitor attractions in their own right, but also have important archives which you may need to use if you are doing in-depth research on your naval ancestors. In all cases it is important to contact them before visiting to discuss your research and to make an appointment.

Fleet Air Arm Museum, RNAS Yeovilton, Ilchester BA22 8HT; tel: 019 3584 0565; www.fleetairarm.com.

As well as having major collections relating to the Fleet Air Arm, the Museum also has many general naval genealogical sources from the 1890s–1920s (see Appendix 2).

Imperial War Museum, Lambeth Road, London SE1 6HZ; tel: 020 7334 3922; www.iwm.org.uk.

The URL for the collections database is www.iwmcollections.org.uk, although it is difficult to use and by no means complete. The Museum collects material for the conflicts since 1914. It has a huge archive and

The Explore History Centre at the Imperial War Museum offers a welcoming atmosphere for anyone wanting to know more about their naval ancestors. (Imperial War Museum)

library (with well over 1,000,000 books), but is not really the place to visit if you are starting out as the basic resources are largely at TNA. You are likely to visit to read memoirs and personal papers deposited by naval personnel. There is also a huge collection of photographs (both official war photos and unofficial pictures deposited by members of the public), oral-history recordings and old films and newsreels. A new addition is the Explore History Centre on the first floor, which is open during the normal museum opening times (including Sundays and bank holidays) and where there is no need to make an appointment. As well as free access to a large number of online resources, it has many reference books for naval history on the open shelves, together with the most comfortable chairs at the Museum!

Liddell Collection, Brotherton Library, University of Leeds, Woodhouse Lane, Leeds LS2 9JT; tel: 011 3343 5518; www.leeds.ac.uk/library/spcoll/liddle.
Collections of memoirs and papers particularly for the First World War, although there is also a little for the Second World War as well.

National Maritime Museum, Romney Road, Greenwich, London SE10 9NF; tel: 020 8312 6565; www.nmm.ac.uk.

The Royal Navy Museum in the Portsmouth Historic Dockyard has an excellent archive and library on all aspects of naval history. (National Museum of the Royal Navy)

In the Caird Library the National Maritime Museum has extensive archives relating to the Royal Navy, its ships and the men who served in them, although the emphasis seems to be increasingly on the civilian Merchant Navy. At the time of writing the Library is only offering a very restricted service prior its reopening in late 2011 in the new Sammy Ofer Wing. The website includes catalogues to the archive and library collections and several useful guides to naval family history. There's also an interesting blog exploring some of the Museum's archives. If you are researching men who served in the eighteenth- and nineteenth-century RN there is a splendid collection of detailed models of ships on show in one of the galleries.

The Naval Historical Branch (and Admiralty Library), 24 Store, PP2, Main Road, HM Naval Base, Portsmouth PO1 3LU.
The NHB works primarily for the MoD and its collections do not have much of immediate interest to family historians, although it is a hugely important resource for naval history in general. A slightly dated webpage about their work is at www.swmaritime.org.uk/article.php?articleid= 553&atype=a.

Royal Marines Museum, Southsea PO4 9PX; tel: 023 9281 9385; www. royalmarinesmuseum.co.uk.
The Museum has extensive archives about the Royal Marines and the men who served in the regiment. The records are unusually well described on the Museum's website (see also Chapter 8).

Royal Naval Museum, HM Naval Base, Portsmouth PO1 3NH; tel: 023 9272 7562; www.royalnavalmuseum.org/research.htm.
The Museum has an extensive Library with perhaps the most important collection of naval archives after TNA, although relatively few records have immediate genealogical value. Exceptions include papers of the RN Benevolent Fund, material relating to the WRNS, extensive collections of charts and plans, and the captains'/ships' registers recording the appointment and transfer of ships' commanders. There is also a huge library of naval books. A catalogue describing the manuscripts once held by the Admiralty Library but now with the Museum is at http://tinyurl.com/6kq26gk. Unfortunately, the Library is in a restricted area and visitors need to make an appointment in advance and then get a pass (and prove their identify) before they visit. The Museum itself tells the story of the Royal Navy, particularly in the eighteenth and nineteenth century, and maintains a website about the Navy's more recent history at www.seayourhistory.org.uk.

Second World War Experience Centre, 1A Rudgate Court, Walton, Wetherby LS23 7BF; tel: 019 3754 1274; www.war-experience.org.
The Centre has a number of collections of memoirs and personal papers from men who served in the Navy during the Second World War.

Royal Navy Submarine Museum, Haslar Jetty Road, Gosport PO12 2AS; tel: 023 9251 0354 ext 226; www.submarine-museum.co.uk.
The Museum's archive has a fine collection of material about submarines and the men who served on them.

The other major service museums may also have the odd item about the Royal Navy:

- National Army Museum, Royal Hospital Road, London SW3 4HT; tel: 020 7730 0717; www.national-army-museum.org.uk.
- RAF Museum, Graeme Park Way, London NW9 5LL; tel: 020 8295 2266; www.rafmuseum.org.uk.

The ship's bell on HMS Belfast. (Simon Fowler)

Museums and Attractions

There are a number of small museums and attractions devoted to ships and seafarers which are worth visiting to get some feel for the lives your ancestors led. A list of some 300 such places is at: http://people.pwf. cam.ac.uk/mhe1000/museums.htm. Those of particular interest for the Royal Navy are detailed below.

Preserved Ships

HMS *Belfast*; http://hmsbelfast.iwm.org.uk. A Second World War destroyer now moored close to London's Tower Bridge.

Mary Rose, HM Naval Base, Portsmouth PO1 3PX; www.maryrose.org. Henry VIII's warship which originally sank in 1545 and its remains were raised in 1982 to huge international interest. At present a temporary museum shows artefacts from the wreck. A new building (which is due to open mid-2012) will also display the hull.

HMS *Unicorn*, Victoria Dock, Dundee DD1 3JA; www.frigateunicorn.org. It is the oldest British warship afloat (technically HMS *Victory* is in dry dock). It was originally launched in Chatham in 1824. Eventually it put into reserve and ended up as a training ship. Most of the fabric is original.

HMS *Victory*, HM Naval Base, Portsmouth PO1 3PX; www.hms-victory.com. Nelson's flagship, built in 1769 and still in commission. There are regular guided tours round the ship which offer a fascinating insight into life on board.

HMS *Warrior*, HM Naval Base, Portsmouth PO1 3PX; www.hmswarrior. org. HMS *Warrior*, launched in 1860 and powered by both steam and sail, was the largest, fastest and most powerful ship of her day.

Other Museums

Explosion! Museum of Naval Firepower, Priddy's Hard Heritage Area, Gosport PO12 4LE; www.explosion.org.uk.
The Museum offers a history of naval ordnance, from gunpowder in the age of sail to Exocet missiles. Displays of small arms, torpedoes, mines, cannon and munitions manufacture. There is a small archive and library.

Nelson Museum and Local History Centre Priory Street, Monmouth NP25 3XA; http://tiny.cc/xke3e.
An impressive collection of memorabilia associated with Nelson.

Plymouth Naval Base Museum, Devonport Naval Base, Devonport, Plymouth PL2 2BG; www.plymouthnavalmuseum.com.
The Museum is only open to pre-booked tour parties, but from their website it looks as if it has an excellent collection.

Royal Naval Patrol Service Association's Museum, Sparrows Nest, Whapload Road, Lowestoft NR32 1XG; www.rnps.lowestoft.org.uk.
Provides a large display of photographs and other memorabilia. Small archives and library. There are limited opening hours.

Other Attractions

Buckler's Hard Maritime Museum, Buckler's Hard Village, Beaulieu, Brockenhurst SO42 7XB; www.bucklershard.co.uk.

This picturesque hamlet on edge of the New Forest was once an important eighteenth-century shipyard. Some cottages now recreate life of the period and the museum displays a model of the village and shipyard at the time.

Chatham Historic Dockyard Dock Road, Chatham ME4 4TY; www.thedockyard.co.uk.
A complex of museum, light industry, shops, a 'Wooden Walls' shipbuilding display, Victorian ropewalk, new gallery of model ships and three warships to explore. There is a small archive and library.

Hartlepool Historic Quay, Jackson Dock, Maritime Ave, Hartlepool TS24 0XZ; www.hartlepoolsmaritimeexperience.com.
Modern re-creation of eighteenth-century seaport quayside, with naval tailor, weapons shops, naval officer's home, gaol, printers, etc. At its heart is HMS *Trincomalee*, a frigate that was built of teak in Bombay in 1817.

Portsmouth Historic Dockyards, Victory Gate, HM Naval Base, Portsmouth PO1 3LJ; www.historicdockyard.co.uk.
Britain's premier maritime attraction offers a complex of major naval attractions and museums, including HMS *Victory*, the *Mary Rose* and the Royal Naval Museum. You pay to visit the museums and other attractions (a ticket is valid for a year), but access to the historic dockyard itself is free. The ticket also includes a boat trip round Portsmouth harbour which offers an opportunity to see the modern Royal Navy.

Old Royal Naval College, King William Walk, Greenwich, London SE10 9LW; www.oldroyalnavalcollege.org.
The visitor centre has displays on the history of the College and pensioners of the former naval hospital.

Marshland Maritime Museum, 206 Main Road, Clenchwarton, King's Lynn PE34 4AA; tel: 015 5376 5530; www.d-boats.co.uk/museum.htm.
Displays over 2,000 items of naval memorabilia from the collections of an enthusiast. The museum is free, but you to have to make an appointment.

Western Approaches Museum, 1–3 Rumford Street, Liverpool L2 8SZ; www.liverpoolwarmuseum.co.uk.
A complex of underground Main Operations Room, Admiral's Office, Teleprinters Station and other parts of the Western Approaches HQ for the Battle of the Atlantic. Limited opening hours.

Finally, if you are in south-west France, I'd recommend a detour to Rochefort-sur-Mer (which lies between Bordeaux and La Rochelle). Rochefort was purpose built as a base for the French Navy in the 1660s away from the prying eyes of the English. Many of the original buildings survive and now form a delightful museum and visitor attraction. Details at www.corderie-royale.com, although the website is only in French.

BIBLIOGRAPHY

There are surprisingly few books on naval genealogy, indeed this guide is the first general guide for nearly a decade. The key book is Bruno Pappalardo's *Tracing Your Naval Ancestors* (Public Record Office, 2002) to which all researchers in this rather murky sea owe an enormous debt. It is a comprehensive and easily understood guide to records at TNA, although it is now slightly dated. Rather more detailed and frankly much less understandable is Nicholas Rodger's *Naval Records for Genealogists* (Public Record Office, 1998). A guide largely designed for academics is Randolph Cook and Nicholas Rodger's *A Guide to Naval Records in The National Archives of the United Kingdom* (Institute of Historical Research/TNA, 2006). It includes public records deposited outside TNA in places such as the National Maritime Museum and,

They also serve. Pete, the ship's cat on HMS Pelorus, *enjoying a rest on deck.* (E. Highams, *Across a Continent in a Man of War* (Westminster Press, 1909))

surprisingly, the Post Office Archives. It also refers to some documents that have strayed from official custody and are now in the British Library, Cambridge University Library or the Bodleian Library, Oxford, and which are known to fill gaps in the public records. In addition, the Imperial War Museum publishes *Tracing Naval Ancestors* (2nd edn, 2006) which gives sources for the twentieth century. And for the Navy of two centuries ago there is Keith Gregson's *Nelson's Navy 1793–1815: Military History Sources for Family Historians* (Federation of Family History Societies, 2006) and an appendix in Brian Lavery's *Royal Tars* (Conway, 2010).

The books listed below can be consulted in the Open Reading Room at Kew and at the various maritime and naval museum libraries. More specialist titles are described in the appropriate chapter above.

In addition TNA and naval museums provide informative research guides and introductory leaflets on researching aspects of naval genealogy which generally can be downloaded free of charge from their websites. TNA guides are mentioned in the appropriate place in the main text.

Medals

Douglas-Morris, Kenneth, *The Naval General Service Medal Roll 1793–1840*, London, 1982

——, *Naval Medals 1793–1856*, London, 1987

——, *Naval Long Service Medals 1830–1990*, London, 1991

——, *Naval Medals 1857–1880*, London, 1994

Duckers, Peter, *British Military Medals*, Pen & Sword, 2009; Peter Duckers has also written an excellent series of booklets for Shire Books on British medals, honours and decorations

The Medals Yearbook, Token Publishing

Spencer, William, *Medals: The Researchers' Guide*, TNA, 2006

Merchant Seamen

Watts, Chris and Watts, Michael, *My Ancestor was a Merchant Seamen*, Society of Genealogists, 2002

Wilcox, Martin, *Fishing and Fishermen: A Guide for Family Historians*, Pen & Sword, 2009

Royal Marines

Brookes, Richard and Taylor, Matthew, *Tracing Royal Marine Ancestors*, Pen & Sword, 2008

Divall, Ken, *My Ancestor was a Royal Marine*, Society of Genealogists, 2008

General Genealogy

Bevan, Amanda, *Tracing Your Ancestors in The National Archives*, 7th edn, TNA, 2006

Fowler, Simon, *Tracing Your Family History*, Pen & Sword, 2011

Spencer, William, *Family History in the Wars*, TNA, 2007

Background Reading

There are a number of published bibliographies that list many of the thousands of books that have been published on British naval history over the years.

Rasor, Eugene L., *English/British Naval History since 1815: A Guide to the Literature*, Garland, 1990

——, *English/British Naval History to 1815: A Guide to the Literature*, Praeger, 2004, available on Google Books

——, *Seaforth Bibliography: A Guide to More than 4,000 Works on British Naval History 55BC–1815*, Pen & Sword, 2007

Ancestors magazine, which is mentioned several times in this book, is no longer published. However, back issues can be obtained from Wharncliffe History Magazines, The Drill Hall, Eastgate, Barnsley S70 2EU or tel: 012 2673 4703; email: carolann@whmagazines.co.uk.

Several specialist publishers of naval history include Chatham and Seaforth (now imprints of Pen & Sword, www.pen-and-sword.co.uk), Conway Publishing (www.anovabooks.com/imprint/Conway) and Maritime Books (www.navybooks.com). Also of interest are Naval & Military Press who publish a few titles of their own, but mainly sell a large range of military books of all kinds at www.naval-military-press.com.

Below is a selection of recent books that should, for the most part, be readily available in bookshops or in your local library.

The Navy in the Eighteenth and Nineteenth Centuries

Adkins, Roy, *Trafalgar – The Biography of a Battle*, Little, Brown, 2005

Adkins, Roy and Lesley, *Jack Tar: Life in Nelson's Navy*, Abacus, 2009

Davies, J. D., *Gentlemen and Tarpaulins — The Officers and Men of the Restoration Navy*, Clarendon Press, 1991

Gardner, James Anthony, *Above and Under Hatches*, 1906, repr. Duckworth, 2000

Lavery, Brian, *Nelson's Navy*, Conway Maritime Press, 1989

——, *Empire of the Seas*, Conway, 2009

——, *Royal Tars: the Lower Deck of the Royal Navy 875–1850*, Conway, 2010

Leech, Samuel, *A Voice from the Main Deck*, 1857, repr. Chatham, 1999

McDonald, Janet, *Feeding Nelson's Navy*, Chatham, 2004

Pope, Dudley, *Life in Nelson's Navy*, Chatham Publishing, 1997

Rasor, Eugene L., *Reform in the Royal Navy: A Social History of the Lower Deck, 1850–80*, Gazelle, 1976

Robinson, William, *Jack Nastyface: Memoirs of an English Seaman*, 1836, repr. Naval Institute Press, 2002

Rodger, N. A. M., *The Wooden Wall*, Collins, 1986

Rogers, Nicholas, *The Press Gang*, Hambledon and London, 2005

Stark, S. J., *Female Tars. Women Aboard Ship in the Age of Sail*, Constable, 1996

Vale, Brian, *A Frigate of King George: Life and Duty on a British Man of War*, Tauris, 2001

See also the novels of Patrick O'Brian and C. S. Forrester

The Twentieth Century

The Great War at Sea, Naval Battles of World War One, Pen & Sword, 2010

Arthur, Max, *Lost Voices of the Royal Navy: Vivid Eyewitness Accounts of Life in the Royal Navy from 1914–1945*, Hodder, 2005

Carew, Anthony, *The Lower Deck of the Royal Navy 1900–39: the Invergordon Mutiny in Perspective*, Manchester UP, 1981

McKee, Christopher, *Sober Men and True: Sailor Lives in the Royal Navy 1900–1945*, Harvard, 2002

Owen, Charles, *Plain Yarns from the Fleet: the Spirit of the Royal Navy During its Twentieth Century Heyday*, Sutton, 1997

Plevy, Harry, *Battleship Sailors: The Fighting Career of HMS 'Warspite' Recalled by Her Men*, Chatham, 2003

Second World War

Barnett, Corelli, *Engage the Enemy More Closely: the Royal Navy in the Second World War*, Penguin Classics, 2000

Lavery, Brian, *Churchill's Navy: the Ships, Men and Organisation 1939–1945*, Conway, 2008

——, *In Which They Served: the Royal Navy Officer Experience in the Second World War*, Conway, 2009

Middlebrook, Martin, *The Sinking of the Prince of Wales & Repulse: The End of a Battleship Era?*, Leo Cooper, 2004

Rossiter, Mark, *Ark Royal: The Life, Death and Rediscovery of the Legendary Second World War Aircraft Carrier*, Corgi, 2007

See also Nicholas Montsarrat's classic novel *The Cruel Sea*

INDEX